Falconry

The Essential Guide

Falconry
The Essential Guide

Steve Wright

THE CROWOOD PRESS

First published in 2006 by
The Crowood Press Ltd
Ramsbury, Marlborough
Wiltshire SN8 2HR

www.crowood.com

This impression 2015

British Library Cataloguing-in-Publication Data
A catalogue record for this book is available from the British Library.

ISBN   978 1 86126 863 1

Disclaimer
The author and the publisher do not accept any responsibility or liability
of any kind in any manner whatsoever for any error or omission, or any
loss, damage, injury or adverse outcome incurred as a result of the use of
any of the information contained in this book, or reliance upon it.

Typeset by NBS Publications, Basingstoke, England.

Printed and bound in India by Replika Press Pvt. Ltd.

Contents

DEDICATION

In remembering the many mistakes I have perpetrated in getting so far, I dedicate this book to my next hawk. Perhaps I will get it right this time.

ACKNOWLEDGEMENTS

This book could not have been written without the help and encouragement of so many good friends. In particular I would like to thank Adrian Jones, Charles Sainsbury-Plaice and my son, Terence Wright, for permitting the use of their photographs and all those clients, friends and falconers who have 'pressed the button' for me at other times. I have been lucky in having access to the birds of Heart of England Falconry and the unstinting help of Richard Wall and his staff, Danielle Shearsby, Bev Beacham, David Fielden, Nikki Cockayne and the boys, Liam, Sam and Richard.

Lastly my sincere thanks go to my partner Sue Connolly for her patience and support throughout the whole endeavour.

Introduction

It has been over a quarter of a century since a bird of prey first sat on my glove. I have been flying and hunting with them ever since, and in that time have trained literally hundreds of people in the sport of falconry. Much of this has been done commercially at my own centre, as have my forays into equipment manufacture, raptor breeding, clearance work and the many other aspects associated with falconry. My summers have been devoted to public displays, while in winter I run hawking experience breaks. Both these activities have brought me in contact with falconers, and would-be falconers, throughout the UK.

This does not mean that I am an expert falconer. Such an animal is impossible to find. One drunken night, a good friend of mine, for whom I have the greatest respect, was putting the world to rights. He asserted, and I believe quite correctly, that 'You can't know a bird until you have hunted with it for at least three years.' Now when I hunt full-time, as I do for six months every winter, I find it virtually impossible to work more than four birds in a day. This means that I would 'learn' a new bird every nine months. Each bird is an individual and there are 280+ species ...

For this reason this book does not claim to be a 'complete treatise on falconry'. What I have set out to do is draw on my own experience to create a common sense guide for the would-be falconer, with signposts to sources of more detailed information where this is appropriate. Much of this handbook's content is centred around the current state of the sport in the UK. This is for two reasons. Firstly, more than 50 per cent of all the falconers in the world are based here. Secondly, we have pressures of space and public attitude putting our sport under threat, which are likely to cause difficulties in other countries in the future.

If reading this handbook gives you a reality check before getting actively involved in falconry, I will have done a service to the sport and the birds themselves. As falconry has become more familiar and accessible, many 'impulse' buyers have bought themselves birds. Every falconry centre has horror stories, where they have had to go in and pick up the pieces afterwards:

'See, I've bought this hawk and it won't eat. What kind of seed should I give it?'

'I bought this peregrine yesterday and let it off in the afternoon. What time will it come back?'

Recognize that, if you cannot do it well, it is better not to do it all. But do not be put off. It may be easy to be a bad falconer, and it may be impossible to be an expert, but it is relatively simple to be a competent one. To become an experienced falconer takes just that, experience. Do not let people over-complicate the theory, stick to common sense and consistency, and have as much pleasure from your birds as my hawks have given me.

Wherever possible I have only used those falconry terms that are met routinely in the falconry world. The more obscure or pretentious words you can find out about yourself. They have an historic interest but, if used today at a modern falconry meeting, would get you some very strange looks. Ours is a growing sport and its followers are suspicious of the poser, whether in a dress or vocabulary sense.

Terms that cause endless confusion are hawk and falcon, as they are capable of more than one definition. In the widest sense I use hawk for any diurnal bird of prey. Similarly I have used falcon to denote a member of the long-winged group of raptors, not, in the narrower way, to describe a female of the above group or, more specifically still, the female peregrine. The spoken word 'falcon' can cause problems too. I find that I swing between two different pronunciations. If you want to say it as 'fawcon' like the French *faucon*, that is correct. If, on the other hand you choose to say it with a hard 'falkon' like the German *falke*, that too is OK. Neither will expose you as an ignorant novice.

Throughout this book I have included anecdotes of events that have happened to me. This has only been done where that particular incident really drove home the lesson to be learnt. In recounting them I hope to underline the message without you having to experience the problem yourself.

CHAPTER 1

Becoming a Falconer

Falconry displays are popular attractions at outdoor events.

Nowadays birds of prey are thrust in front of the public at every conceivable opportunity. There cannot be a school that has not received an educational visit from a falconry or raptor rehabilitation centre. Equally every outdoor event seems to have its flying or static display.

It was not always like this. In the 1950s and 60s pesticide poisonings had all but wiped out our native birds of prey. There was an urgent need to publicize their plight and to educate landowners and farmers in their conservation. To achieve this the falconers of the day staged displays at county and agricultural shows. Inadvertently this also advertised, to a wider public, the continued existence of the sport and set in motion our ongoing love affair with the birds. It is useless to speculate on whether or not the displays were a good thing. They happened and modern-day falconry resulted from it.

Such an exhibition was my first contact with the sport, as I suspect it was yours, and it is a misleading one. Displays are not falconry – they are a demonstration of the principles of training and exercising hawks and falcons. The true sport consists of taking quarry with birds of prey. It was, and remains, a pragmatic way of putting food on the table. Only with the advent of 'fowling pieces' (round about the time of the Wars of the Roses in the fifteenth century for the history buffs), did it become primarily a sport.

Broadly speaking everybody gets drawn to falconry by a combination of the following:

- A visual attraction to the birds. They are beautiful and have an emotive image.
- A romantic vision of the sport. The falconer can seem a free spirit, enviably at one with nature and possessed of uncanny power over wild creatures.
- The historical connection. We have a tendency to view the past through rose-coloured spectacles. The esoteric language of falconry (which you will not find in this book), the pageantry, the decorative hoods and gauntlets, and the social role of the sport make it attractive in our modern, high-tech world.
- The hunting ethos. Some of us have a love for hunting of all kinds and are drawn to explore falconry as an extension of this side of our experience.
- Self-image. For some people the possession of a bird of prey confers 'machismo', rather in the way that owning a Rottweiler does.

Each of the above desires can be satisfied in other ways. Wanting to be a falconer is not reason enough to go out and buy a falcon, so before leaping in, try to satisfy your needs with the following:

- Visit falconry centres, take photographs, buy some of the many excellent artworks that are available (falconry is well served by many extremely talented artists).
- Get real. The falconer is burdened with legislation and restrictions and is permanently fretting about the health, weight and performance of his or her bird. And it is hard to feel romantic about sitting under a tree in winter with icy water trickling down your neck, waiting for your bird to dry out or become hungry enough to come

down to you. Especially when you are late for work or the bird is about to be cited as a reason for divorce.

- Despite its roots falconry is a modern, evolving sport. The average falconer is more interested in microtransmitters, radio technology, vitamin supplements and DNA testing than in thirteenth-century legislation relating to the ownership of 'ye hawkes'.
- By all means go out hawking. Most falconry centres can arrange hunting trips with their birds, where you get to handle them in the field. But, unlike a gun or a fishing rod, the hawk requires daily attention – and they can live for a long time. To paraphrase the National Canine Defence League's excellent sticker, 'A hawk is for life, not just for Christmas.'

But what if your interest persists? Are there different levels of involvement that would be better suited to your own motivation and circumstances? You may not have enough time or access to sufficient hawking land to be able to hunt with a bird of your own. Instead you could become a **hawk keeper**, giving a caring home to an injured bird of prey. There is a continuing demand for responsible homes for rescued individuals that are unable to be returned to the wild. Sometimes falconers need homes for their pensioners, birds that through injury or disability are no longer able to hunt effectively.

Alternatively you may have no desire to hunt quarry but simply wish to enjoy flying a hawk, owl or falcon for pleasure. This is looked down upon by some falconers but it is really no different from owning a border collie and not rounding up sheep: you can still do obedience, agility, flyball or whatever with the dog. As long as your pet is exercised mentally and physically, and you get pleasure from the arrangement, it is a good deal all round. Most birds of prey would not miss hunting as such, and will happily become dependent on you if allowed to. It should not come as a surprise. How many of us have gone grubbing for roots and berries in preference to going to the local supermarket? The dilemma in becoming a **hawk flyer**, as opposed to a **falconer**, is that your bird may not be able to hunt for itself if (or more probably, bearing in mind the nature of the beast, when) it gets lost. On the other hand, it will probably be very tame, eventually appearing on someone's rooftop or in their garden, so that it will be more easily found and recovered. In contrast the falconer's bird will cope comfortably by itself, but will quickly become too wild and fat to return.

Before getting a hawk, owl or falcon (I am leaving eagles out of this as they are not beginners' birds), the aspiring falconer should delay as long as possible. He or she is recommended to:

- Visit as many falconry centres, and watch as many displays by different people, as possible.
- Take whatever courses are available. There will be good and bad courses but all will be run by enthusiasts and even the worst will be better than no training at all.
- Join a local falconry club and attend field meetings.
- Get to know local falconers, try to go out with them and perhaps help by looking after their bird while they are on holiday. Be prepared to be a beater or ferret boy, and do not be surprised if you are not welcomed with open arms. Falconers can get fed up with people trying to participate in what is essentially a solitary and private hobby.
- Go on hawking days with a professional falconer, via your local centre.

HOW DO I BECOME A FALCONER?

When you have decided that you want to start the sport, having put it off as long as you can, you must then ask yourself if you are able to follow it. Do you have the following:

Desire
Yes, you have proved that by persisting in your interest.

Time
Be realistic about this. It may dictate if you become a hawk keeper, a hawk flyer or a falconer.

Caring for injured birds in an aviary takes only a few minutes a day, and they can safely be left with enough food to last them a couple of days if you have to go away. Getting someone to feed them for longer periods is not impossible, but make sure they are reliable.

Flying a hawk, owl or falcon takes as long as the bird's appetite lasts. Once it has eaten enough it will terminate the lesson of its own accord. You must ensure that this happens on your fist, and not on someone's roof or up an unclimbable tree! You are, or should be, in control of the situation and can make the exercise period as long or short as you need. Also your bird does not need to be as fit as a hunting bird, so it does not matter if you have to miss a day or two – provided this is not a regular occurrence. When you find the regular flights are too time consuming, you should reassess whether you would not be better being a hawk keeper.

To actively hunt with a bird takes a lot of time. Unless you can budget at least one hour of daylight a day, five days a week, in the winter, you are being over-optimistic. In fact you would always want more than this. The reality is that we all have less time than we think, and other people make demands on it. Ideally you need to be unemployed, self-employed, retired, or a part-time or shift-worker. Anyone with a nine-to-five, five-day-a-week job will find it almost impossible to do.

Falconry is a selfish sport. It takes us away from our family and friends. It may intrude on our work also. When I had a proper job I found it was possible, in the winter, to fly my bird before I went to work. This involved breakfasting in the dark and driving out to the local woods in time for first light. If I was disciplined enough I could get a quick forty-five minutes into the bird and still get to work on time. Many times I arrived in hunting gear, with the bird in the back of the car. It became used to being perched outside my office window.

Sometimes it might, however, take a bath and sit high in a tree, hanging its wings out to dry. It couldn't be left there as, once it was airworthy again, it would commence hunting, and might then be unrecoverable. The required course of action was to stay with it. The first time this occurred my boss was more amused than bothered. As an excuse I suspect this was a rather novel one. A few weeks later we were late again. 'Does this sort of thing happen often?' I was asked. 'Only twice,' I replied. By the fourth time relations were a bit less cordial.

When you have a 'proper job' you look forward to the weekends. At last there are lumps of time and you might be able to devote a whole morning or afternoon to hawking. Of course the garden has not been dug and the hall is undecorated, but let it go. To pacify management you have agreed to visit the in-laws for Sunday lunch. Then the bird goes AWOL. Perhaps it has been frightened by a dog or a mountain bike (other folk use the great outdoors at weekends too) or it has killed a squirrel up a tall, and visibly unsafe, tree. At any rate you know the Sunday roast is charring in the mother-in-law's oven, and she is sticking pins into the effigy of you which she keeps specifically for that purpose.

Andy was an excellent falconer and flew his much-loved hawk with great success for many seasons. Marriage, to an understanding woman, was no hindrance until, in the way of these things, children came along. At the same time he achieved promotion and started working longer hours. He gave the hawk to me with great regret, having sensibly decided that he could not justify the time he spent on the bird, nor could he justify keeping it and not flying it. 'If my circumstances change I'll have it back,' he told me. 'Otherwise I'll wait till the kids are older before I get another one.' Not everyone is so responsible.

So, when calculating the time you have available, please remember the other demands there will be on it. You can always take occasional days out with a centre or with your local club.

Facilities

You will need the following:

- A secure shed or outbuilding of some kind for overnight accommodation.
- A secure area for the hawk to be put out to 'weather' each day.
- Or a large and secure aviary that combines the two above functions.
- Permitted access to substantial areas of land that hold adequate, suitable game.

A Financial and Emotional Budget

Falconry is not an expensive hobby once the initial set-up costs have been met. However, there may be veterinary expenses (exotic birds get exotic bills) and even replacement costs for lost hawks. This last item, which includes death and injury, requires an emotional budget from you. 'If you have livestock you have dead stock' is a very true saying. Birds of prey, like all predators, are risk takers and have a violent lifestyle, and seem to spend much of their time inventing new ways to kill themselves. You cannot protect them from everything, anymore than you should stop your children climbing trees. The death of a hawk is devastating, but bear in mind that the captive hawk will almost certainly have lived longer and died more peacefully than it ever would in the wild.

There are insurance policies that cover birds of prey against veterinary costs, loss when flying, death, loss of use and third party liability.

The Will to Hunt

Yours should be an unholy alliance. If one or the other of you is not fully committed to hunting then you will not catch game. You will need to study the lie of the land, using cover, contours and wind direction to maximize your chances of success. Frequently novice falconers are slow to enter their hawks to game, as their first priority is to consolidate the bird's training. Continuous obedience training may make the bird too dependent on you, however, and if it is then given impossible slips, for example upwind or uphill, it will see no point in pursuing quarry that is obviously unattainable. Instead it will return to the fist, where a nice reward awaits it. Before long it will become a pacifist.

Training and Guidance

The level of competence that is required to own a bird is open to debate. Some countries have a statutory requirement, and this varies according to the individual government. Other countries, particularly in the developing world, have no legislation at all concerning birds of prey. In the UK anyone may purchase a captive bred bird of prey (birds of wild origin are never normally encountered except where they are being rehabilitated or are permanently disabled, so may be ignored for these purposes). Sadly there is no requirement to achieve or prove any level of competence. The birds have no more protection than a budgerigar in a pet shop.

UK falconry is fortunate in that we have a lot of falconry centres throughout the country. In 2005 there were thirty-eight listed, most of them providing tuition. The courses vary from half-day modules, which when added together can constitute a complete course, to a selection of longer courses. My own preference is for the modular system. I feel you need to

> ### Falconry Training in the US
>
> In North America there is an effective apprenticeship programme which is monitored, on behalf of the government, by the North American Falconers Association (NAFA). Entry into an apprenticeship is rigorously controlled, and there is both a practical and theoretical examination before qualification. This has contributed to the slow rate of growth of falconry in North America, but as a result the standard of skills in the sport are good.
>
> Similar schemes exist, for example, in Germany, Spain, Zimbabwe and South Africa. Most countries permit birds to be taken from the wild, but only under licence. For contact details of overseas falconry organizations please refer to www.ibr.org.uk.

learn at a pace that suits you, returning for more when it is appropriate or you are capable of absorbing more information. The longer courses can give you information overload, resulting in reduced understanding.

The standard of these courses varies wildly, as does the competence of the people giving them. Some are properly structured and presented by qualified trainers, while others are marketed by cowboys. When I first started running courses myself (I hasten to add that I *am* a qualified training manager), one of my early clients opened a centre within a few weeks of taking his first module. He would reappear at intervals for further tuition when he had clients waiting to do the next module! Another falconer advertised courses from his 'hawking school' within a year of getting his first bird.

Even reputable centres may not provide what you are looking for. One well-established, and deservedly respected, school runs longer courses. Their five-day beginners course involves manning a bird (that is, carrying it on the fist), for two hours each day. As this process can be readily taught in about twenty minutes, this does not strike me as cost-effective training. However, viewed as part of a falconry-related holiday, it is quite acceptable.

Choosing what course to go on is therefore a potential banana skin. Speak to the falconers giving public displays and assess their apparent level of knowledge and their readiness to share it. Also ask your local falconry club whom they would recommend. At the end of the day any course is better than none at all.

There are so many falconers in the UK that you may have someone who will undertake to supervise you. Again try to establish the competence of your proposed instructor. We do come across some very indifferent 'advisors'. Some of the bigger falconry clubs in the UK run structured apprenticeship schemes. These are a good idea but depend on volunteers to make them work. In practice this means that the availability of good guidance can be hit or miss depending on where you live.

Personally I would like to see an agreed syllabus, with an examination to validate the training given. There is no reason why, with so many falconry centres, it should not be possible for these exams (both practical and theoretical) to be commercially available. Rather like MOT garages, the examining centres would have to be of proven reputation, and this would, in turn, enhance the overall standard of course provision.

A word of caution is needed, however. Two clients of mine had both taken all my course modules over a matter of years. They had also been on extended hunting trips with me, and had become so proficient that I was happy to let them set off on their own, with my birds and dogs. They recognized that their lifestyles were not compatible with being a falconer, so contented themselves with regular 'fixes' with me.

One became self-employed while the other took early retirement. Suddenly they had the time and flexibility to own a hawk of their own. I believed that they were both more than competent, and had no hesitation in supplying them with young, untrained, female Harris hawks. In fairness to them, both have achieved success, but they also said how much more difficult it was than they expected. Working other people's trained birds is very different from making that decision to fly the bird free for the first time, or even deciding if it is at its best flying weight.

CHAPTER 2

Choosing a Bird

There are over 280 species of diurnal raptor and more than 150 owls. The choice seems endless, and you can end up like a child in a sweetshop. Too many people let their hearts rule their heads and end up buying a completely inappropriate bird. This helps nobody, and the one to suffer most is always the hawk. It is important to analyse your needs dispassionately, and it will then become clear that the choice is surprisingly limited. The considerations to be borne in mind are:

- The habitat/countryside you will be flying in.
- The quarry species that are available to you.
- Your preference and pocket.

Having identified these you must then list those species that match your requirements. This, if you intend hunting, will be a narrower choice than you might think. For hawk flyers, as opposed to falconers, the list is much more extensive, because only the first and third elements need to be catered for. The birds themselves divide into five groups:

- The long-winged falcons.
- The broad-winged buteos and eagles.
- The short-winged accipiters.
- Owls.
- Kites, vultures and other scavengers.

To help you understand the constraints you will be under, we can look at all these points in greater detail.

HABITAT/COUNTRYSIDE

Wooded Countryside
Woodland and enclosed, hedged landscapes account for most of the southern half of Britain and a substantial amount of the north as well. In dense woodland a bird needs to be a good short-distance sprinter and very manoeuvrable. This would rule out the long-winged falcons, which are built to be missiles and need half the county to turn round in, but would favour the accipiters (true hawks like goshawks and sparrowhawks). As woods give way to increasingly larger fields and isolated copses the need is less for agility and more for sustained flight. Here the buteos (buzzard types), particularly the woodland fringe dwellers, are at an advantage.

There are practical difficulties to consider. Woodland and hedgerows limit your range of vision and slow down your attempts to keep up with your hawk. A bird of prey does not have to go very far to be out of sight. Once you have lost visual contact with it you will have to assume that it will continue in the direction that you last saw it taking, but in woodland it may not be easy to keep to that direction yourself. Quite a small deviation from your intended route may cost you time in locating your missing bird.

Also the quarry has not got to go far to find cover in which to hide, so unless your bird has the pace to get close to it before it reaches sanctuary, the chances are that it will miss its prey. Remember the quarry is on its own territory and knows every bit of cover that exists.

Open Ground

This can consist of marsh or estuary, prairie, downland, moors or mountains. Very flat, open farmland, such as you might find in parts of East Anglia, may also qualify. Here game can see you from a distance and is wary, so your bird of prey needs to have long-range potential. This is primarily falcon country but, since you and your fist provide a moving tree from which to launch the fist-held hawks, they too can perform in such an environment.

In open country the terrain is critical. High hills give your bird lift and good vantage spots. This means they can, and will, take on long chases. Are you fit enough to follow? Telemetry (radio tracking gear) may enable you to retrieve your hawk, but you may get little pleasure out of the exercise. Buteos, accipiters and eagles work relatively closely (!) but falcons can go a devilish distance. So,

for example, do not attempt grouse hawking on hill country unless you are very fit.

QUARRY SPECIES

We will look at the advantages and disadvantages of the various species later on, but they fall into two categories: ground game and flying game. Some birds of prey are versatile and will take both while others are more specific in their hunting needs. Size counts and, although both types prefer to take ground game, you would not attempt to take a roe deer with a kestrel or use a golden eagle to take a mouse. Similarly a male sparrowhawk (properly called a musket) would be adept at taking small garden birds but would be over-faced if asked to tackle prey more suited to a gyr falcon, such as geese. Having said that, I just know someone is going to tell me about their musket, which regularly takes out swans and light aircraft!

I have purposely avoided the less common species and have concentrated on the hunting birds most commonly used. Beginners are unlikely to start with anything very exotic.

Game Species and Where They are to be Found				
	Large flying game: hen pheasant, rook upwards	Small flying game: partridge to skylark	Large ground game: roe, fox, hare	Small ground game: rabbit, squirrel
Open hill	Large long-winged falcons: saker, gyr, peregrine, prairie, hybrids. Male and female gos	Merlin, small males of the large falcon species and barbary, lanner, lugger and so on	Eagles, female red-tails, hawk eagles, ferruginous, female gos, female Harris	Male and female gos, male and female red-tails, male and female Harris
Open flat land	As above	Small long-winged falcons and tiercels, merlin, sparrowhawk	As above	As above
Woodland edge	Male and female gos, red-tail, Harris	Sparrowhawk, Cooper's hawk	Female red-tail, gos, Harris	Male and female gos, red-tail, Harris
Dense woodland	As above	As above	As above	As above

COMMON FALCONRY BREEDS

For falconry purposes, birds of prey can be divided into three groups, according to their conformation. These differences are not based on size but on relative body weight, the design of their wings and the proportion of wing in relation to their tail. Understanding why these variations have developed will help you appreciate why you have to purchase a bird that is suitable for the area and game you have available.

The Longwings

These are the falcons. Their basic habitat is open countryside. Lacking the advantage of trees to use as look-out posts their main vantage point for seeking game has to be the sky. Like all predators they are lazy and, to conserve energy, have developed long, narrow, pointed wings so that they resemble feathered gliders. Using these they can ride the air currents and thermals with minimum effort. The higher they climb, the wider the area they can search for their prey. It is not unusual for falcons to attain heights of a few thousand metres – provided the thermals will lift them up there.

From this 'hunting pitch' they can see for miles, but they are also a long way from any intended quarry. Here their elongated wings are a disadvantage because, being such long levers, they cannot be moved quickly. This prevents falcons from accelerating readily. They get round this by folding their wings tightly to their bodies and falling. In a stoop, with their super-streamlined shape eliminating drag, they can achieve speeds of over 480kph (300mph) – fast enough to catch up with the fastest quarry. They are exercised and trained to a swung lure.

I once had the good fortune to fly my birds in an arena beside which was a huge, 13m (40ft)-high television screen. A cameraman filmed each display and the audience could watch the enlarged birds on the screen. One of my falcons chose to go up on a thermal. It was a hot day and the bird went up until it was only a tiny speck in the sky. On the big screen we could all see it clearly as it circled lazily around, its head scanning from side to side. When I called it down, it folded

Falcon's wings are designed for gliding, and are narrow and pointed.

Falcon's feet – designed for bird-catching.

Falcon's head with notched beak and dark eyes.

everything flat and dropped like a stone. It was lost from sight to the naked eye, but on our giant screen we could see it close up – a privilege you would never normally have. It was totally streamlined, as sleek and smooth as the barrel of a dart, and we could see the clouds flickering past as it shot down. After a while it seemed to change its profile slightly, becoming more bulky. Without its wings extending in any way from its body it slowed markedly. The clouds passed more steadily. Eventually it stuck out its wing 'butts', the merest extension of its shoulders, and again lost speed. Following this the wings came half open, and its feet dropped down into attack mode. At this point I looked up and the bird was still a couple of hundred feet above me, and coming in like a jet plane.

As an attacking technique the falcon has obviously found that being a feathered missile is rather effective. However, its success depends on outright speed, so that steering and brakes are of less importance. The falcon dares not risk hitting ground game, as the impact would be too great, and it also lacks the manoeuvrability to catch running quarry. Birds in flight are a different matter and the falcon has developed long, slender toes, for

tensile strength, to wrap around its feathered victims.

All falcons can be recognized by their long, scimitar-shaped wings, which cross over each other in repose. The second primary (the feather next to the last one in the wing) is the longest, and makes the extended wing appear to be pointed.

They also all have dark and very round eyes, and a small notch towards the tip of their beak. The latter is supposed to aid them in breaking their victim's neck, but I have yet to know a bird of prey with humane impulses. My personal belief is that this shape is caused by a weakness, where the beak grows around either side of the nares (nostrils). These are particularly large in falcon species and, if a beak becomes overgrown, it is always here that it will split. Captive falcons are kept on block perches as they prefer to stand on flat surfaces.

As always there are exceptions. Female saker falcons can be used for ground game, although this is a waste of a bird and they are not as good as hawks and eagles. Conversely the New Zealand falcon lives in forested areas and can hunt like a hawk. It has short (but still pointed) wings and a comparatively long tail to give it this manoeuvrability, although it is certainly ready to stoop if the opportunity arises.

A peregrine falcon on a pheasant. They are bird-catching specialists. (© Agripix Ltd)

Kestrels are a whole group of very specialized falcons. They have evolved to still-hunt out of the sky in enclosed areas. Their long tail gives them balance and added surface area, and enables them to check in their descent. This control allows them to catch ground game. Unlike most falcons the kestrel has short, sturdy feet that can stand up to impact with the ground.

Peregrine (Falco peregrinus)

This is the definitive falcon. Peregrines are widespread throughout the world and are now virtually at pest level in some areas. To hunt successfully with one you will need telemetry and a trained, pointing dog of some sort. The falcon is swift and powerful, with the tiercel (male) being smaller and more nimble than its mate. Both sexes have calm temperaments but they have a great drive to hunt and can still disappear. Anyone hunting with a peregrine needs access to very open land.

They are often hybridized with gyr falcons and other large species such as the saker and prairie falcon. As with most birds of prey, the larger female costs more than the male, and market pressure from the Arab states and Spain has made prices rise.

Prairie (Falco mexicanus)

This is a North American falcon with attitude, which readily flies at a high pitch but is also wayward. It is slightly lighter in weight than the peregrine but compensates with aggression. It will take on a wide range of flying quarry and recently North American falconers have tried working them in conjunction with lurchers to catch jack rabbits.

The saker is a desert falcon and is widely used in the Arab world.

Although an African species, the lanner falcon has been known in Britain for many centuries.

Barbary (Falco pelegrinoides)

A small sub-species of the peregrine that tends to be more confiding. It is very agile and obedient, but is not often offered for sale.

Saker (Falco cherrug)

Beloved by Arab falconers, this is a large and fast desert falcon. It will hunt ground or flying game in the wild, but is used for grouse, rook and partridge in the UK. The Arabs use them in relays to catch desert hares and the houbara (McQueen's bustard). Classically they were also trained to work with their masters' salukis in pursuit of antelope. Their role was to strike at the beast's eyes until it slowed up enough for the saluki to overtake and kill it.

Sakers can be very obedient but they can become unreliable in spring and autumn, as they are a migratory species, so telemetry is a must. Females are much sought after for clearance work and will tackle gulls and crows with zeal. Blonde individuals are more popular but this has no bearing on working ability.

Lanner (Falco biarmicus)

This medium-sized falcon is popular as a display bird, particularly the males (lannerets), who are sharper and more agile. It will take partridge, pigeon, duck and even magpie in open areas. Most lanners are gentle and easy to train, but they have a tendency to soar and are often lost as a result. There are several recognized sub-species, based on distribution, size, colour and markings. The price is the same for both sexes.

Lugger (Falco jugger)

This small but powerful falcon is on the red list of endangered species. It does not have a good reputation as a hunting bird although individuals have done well. A longish tail gives improved manoeuvrability and brakes and luggers have quite large and sturdy feet. It's no surprise that they take lizards off the walls in their native India. Despite their rarity they are not expensive to buy as they are not in great demand.

Merlin (Falco columbarius)

Traditionally this was considered to be the ladies' falcon because of its small size, which makes it delicate and therefore unsuitable for novices. They are flown at skylarks, but the necessary quarry licences for these are getting harder to obtain. Merlins are pretty little birds, and quickly become tame and confiding. They are very fast and agile, and can really test your ability to exercise them to a swung lure. At one time I flew two merlins together (a cast); it was furiously fast work and they could virtually turn me inside out. The males (jacks) are tiny and a totally different colour to their mates.

Merlins were thought to be less active as adult birds and were traditionally released back to the wild at the end of a brief skylark season. Now, because of the cost of captive-bred birds, they are retained over the winter. This has led to the discovery that their failure to achieve good results as their quarry got older was due to the latter having a lighter body weight in the early autumn. It was this that gave the larks the edge, not any reduction in the falcon's ability. Later on in the winter the larks got heavier and the merlin was once again able to outfly them.

Merlins are difficult to breed in captivity and are correspondingly expensive. I think they are worth every penny, but novices really should not inflict themselves on such delicate birds. Anyone contemplating owning a merlin should read *A Merlin for Me* by John Loft.

The merlin is Britain's smallest falcon and traditionally flown by ladies at skylarks.

Kestrel (Falco tinnunculus)

This is the commonest British falcon. Kestrels are successful in the wild because they are very versatile – they will take mice, voles, insects, small birds, earthworms and carrion. Their nest may be a simple scrape on a ledge of a quarry or building, or they can take over old crow's nests or, perhaps, lay their eggs in a hole in a tree.

In captivity they can be flown to the fist or a swung lure and, although not generally viewed as a proper hunting bird, will sometimes take birds as big as starlings. They are mostly charming pets that will stay around your garden during the day. In captivity they rarely hover well (why bother with such hard work

The humble kestrel was known as the windhover for its individual style of flight.

Hybrid falcons are increasingly being produced for falconry.

when they know where the food is), but they do improve with the passage of time. Most new falconers move on to something else before then, so kestrels rarely reach their full potential.

Their small size makes them vulnerable to weight loss, so they are not really recommended as a beginner's bird. However they are tougher than merlins, hobbies or sparrowhawks. Before trying one of these species you would be well advised to learn weight control on a kestrel first. My personal experience is that kestrels seem to 'wed' to whatever they are first flown to, that is, a kestrel trained to the fist will always prefer that to a lure, while conversely a lure-trained kestrel seems to have little interest in coming to the fist. If a kestrel learns to go up high it can put in an impressive stoop and, with such a large tail, can stop at the last minute.

Hybrid Falcons

Nowadays there are a bewildering variety of hybrid falcons produced commercially. The reasons given for this 'fashion' are varied. It is suggested that there is a political justification, in that the hybrid breeders are creating domestic breeds. Should our sport ever be attacked by the anti-hunting lobbby (and it is probable that we will not escape their attention), we are unlikely to be forced to release artificially created, 'mongrel' breeds into the wild. Equally the existence of hybrids may mean that in future there will be no need to take wild-bred native birds.

There are also arguments for hybridizing on health grounds. In the wild possibly as few as 20 per cent of birds of prey reach breeding age, as they are subject to the most rigorous process of natural selection. Our captive birds do not benefit (or suffer) from this, and in fact it is often the injured ones that end up in breeding projects. Almost by definition this argues that our captive breeding stock is gradually deteriorating in quality (although there is no hard evidence available to support this suspicion). Continued breeding of pure-bred members of the same species could result in the production of poor quality, sub-standard progeny. This is where the hybrids are thought to be better. They are believed to possess hybrid vigour and to be more robust and hardy.

The practice of hybridizing falcons began really as a result of frustration. For centuries falconers have coveted gyr falcons, the largest of all the longwings and obtainable in a mouth-watering range of colours. Unfortunately the birds, coming from the arctic, did not thrive in more temperate conditions; their respiratory systems were unable to resist infection and they died prematurely. By crossing them with peregrines and sakers, it was hoped to retain much of the size of the gyr, but add in some of the toughness of the other species. This worked and encouraged further, occasionally bizarre, experimentation. I have even seen a hybrid between a peregrine and a tiny, American kestrel.

Some species of a similar size will hybridize naturally but others can only be bred with artificial insemination. Natural hybrids have been known to occur in the wild, and DNA evidence suggests that they have been absorbed into the gene pool of at least one of the pure species.

Having been brought up to believe that a species could be defined as one that, crossed with another related species, was unable to produce fertile offspring, I find it unsettling that hybrid falcons can not only be fertile, but that they can be bred to a third species yet again. As a result you can buy 'trybrids' and possibly even more complicated crosses. All these fertile crosses may cause genetic pollution in the future. Additionally it seems to me that we are failing to identify, and breed from, our very best pure-breds. Surely, with

The common buzzard, a typical broadwing and the commonest bird of prey in Britain.

man's record for selective breeding, we are capable of developing superior, domestic strains of the natural species.

The Broadwings

Nature abhors a vacuum, and where there is quarry there will be predators. While the falcons specialize in taking other birds in open areas, the same land is home to ground game. This may be as big as roe deer, fox, hare, rabbit and, in North America, various ground squirrels and prairie dogs. All these are relatively heavy for their size and the bird of prey needs to be similarly built to hold them. Flying over open land they will still need to mount up in the air in search of food, but narrow falcon wings would not carry their weight. Equally the game is slower than flying quarry so the broadwings need not be as streamlined.

This is where the eagles, hawk eagles and buteos come into their own. Their wings have a large surface area to carry their bulk on updraughts and thermals. Because they may hit the earth with some force, their feet are usually very strong. In relation to the size of their victims the toes are short, because rather than grasping their prey, the broadwing uses its weight to pin it down on the ground.

Some broadwings can, and will, operate in wooded areas. For the most part, however, their efficiency depends on them having space to operate. I have seen a trained golden eagle hunting in a forest, but it was a very open one, with well-spaced, mature trees.

Eagles are generally larger and heavier than the hawk eagles and buzzards, and are not for beginners! The first bird of prey I was ever offered was an eagle and I am very glad I had the good sense to recognize my limitations.

Eagles

Golden Eagle (Aquila chrysaetos)
The finest of the eagles, the golden eagle can be used for hunting hare, fox and even roe deer. The related berkut, or imperial, eagle is used on wolf. Eagles can be difficult and dangerous, and are heavy to carry – males weigh 2.75–3.5kg (6–8lb) and females 4–5.5kg (9–12lb). You need access to huge tracts of open country.

Verreaux or Black Eagle (Aquila verreauxii)
This huge species has impressive feet and is reputedly a bit easier to handle than the goldie.

Steppes and Tawny Eagles (Aquila nipalensis and A. rapax)
These are smaller than the above species and tend to be less courageous in the hunting field. The weight ranges from 2.25kg (5lb) for males to 3.5kg (8lb) for females.

Hawk Eagles
A halfway stage in size, the hawk eagles are interesting birds not met with frequently. Species include Bonelli's (Hieraaetus fasciatus), Hodgson's (Spizaetus nipalensis). They are often forest species and are quite manoeuvrable.

Hybrid Eagles
As with falcons there are sometimes hybrid eagles produced. There seems to be no

justification for this other than that the breeder had two birds available of different species. Possibly there is a very limited gene pool in some species that makes such a complete out-cross desirable.

Buteos (Buzzards)
Buzzards are fairly limited birds because of their inherent laziness, but are often recommended for the beginner, who must develop good fieldcraft skills with this family. The buteos lack the speed and flair of the falcons, and the dash and agility of the accipiters, so are seen as being somehow unglamorous. Nevertheless they are very hardy and long-lived, and will fulfil the basic criterion of a bird of prey, which is to put food on the table. Imprinted buzzards of all species are noisy and spiteful, and are best avoided. (American readers may be confused by the name buzzard, as that is what they call their Turkey vulture.)

Common Buzzard (Buteo buteo)
The common (Eurasian) buzzard is the commonest British bird of prey. It is very sluggish and unlikely to catch heavy bags. If you can take double figures of game in one season with a buzzard you are certainly ready for something better. Sexing them can be difficult, as the male offspring of a large pair may easily be bigger than a female bred from smaller parents. The range of colours, from nearly pure white to reddish or chocolate brown, produces some very attractive individuals. Older birds are fairly easily obtained, but their low value means that few people bother to breed them nowadays and youngsters are hard to come by.

The buzzard was the beginner's bird in Europe until the invasion of the North American hawks began in the 1960s. They had the advantages of being common and very hardy. The two most frequent mistakes made by novices are to either overfeed or underfeed their bird. The first fault normally results in the hawk or falcon flying away,

Red-Tailed Buzzard or Red-Tailed Hawk in the US (Buteo jamaicensis)

This is a much larger and more aggressive bird than its European cousin (with which it will interbreed). It is a bona fide hunting bird with the requisite qualities of hardiness, robustness and courage. Some American falconers hunt several together in groups! It is powerful but not very manoeuvrable – launching a red-tail at quarry has all the subtlety of throwing a rock. This is not meant to be derogatory in any way. The red-tail goes in like a ton of bricks, and woe betide anything it gets its talons into. Its tough feet make it a good squirrel bird but big females readily take on hare and can weigh up to 1.8kg (4lb).

Like the common buzzard, the red-tail is long-lived and comes in a wide range of sizes. Falconers in the US identify several different sub-species, such as the Harlan's hawk, based on geographical distribution and colour variations.

In the UK, the red-tail is less frequently bred now that the Harris hawk is so readily available. It does have its enthusiasts, who appreciate its aggression and power.

Ferruginous Buzzard or Ferruginous Hawk in the US (Buteo regalis)

This is often considered as a beginner's eagle, but its small feet are very buzzard-like. Large and impressive, the ferruginous can become very obedient. For a broad-winged bird it has an unusually pointed, falcon-like wing and is able to stoop at speed – yet still hit ground game because of its thick, stubby feet. It comes from the Rocky Mountains and flies best in open country with hills for lift. The ferruginous can eat at a tremendous speed, and must be found quickly or it will gorge on a kill. Some imprinted individuals can be very spiteful towards their handler. They are not often bred as there is little demand for them.

The Shortwings

If you need real manoeuvrability and early acceleration you have to consider that neurotic

The red-tailed hawk is a tough and uncompromising hunter. It is often the beginner's bird for American falconers.

never to be seen again. The buzzard simply flies into the nearest tree, and sits there for days until it is hungry enough to come back to you. On the other hand, if you underfeed a hawk you run the risk it will end up on its back with its feet in the air. Our lowly old buzzard has such a frugal economy that it is virtually impossible to starve one to death. Finally, having failed to lose or kill his buzzard through ignorance, the novice could release it back to the wild. Then he would find that his facilities and equipment were of exactly the right size and dimensions for a goshawk.

The sparrowhawk is the definitive shortwinged hawk.

group, the true accipiters. Most usually these would be the goshawk, sparrowhawk or Cooper's hawk (American readers may be confused by sparrowhawk, as this is the name they commonly give to the diminutive, but feisty, American kestrel. The Eurasian sparrowhawk is halfway between the Cooper's hawk and the sharpshin.) All these hawks live at a million kilometres an hour. It is hard for us to begin to comprehend the speed of their reflexes or their metabolic rate: they burn up calories so fast that they can easily exhaust their blood sugar and suffer a hypoglycaemic fit.

This 'quick-twitch' temperament is necessary for a bird that is a reactive hunter. While they will seek game by cruising opportunistically through woods or over fields, they also still-hunt from favourite perches. In both cases they take quarry by surprise. Because they must hunt over short distances, in enclosed areas, they have short wings that they can move very rapidly, to obtain good early pace, and a huge tail to give superior steering. I have watched my sparrowhawk chase a robin round and round the trunk of an apple tree at full speed. No other bird of prey could have sustained such explosive effort.

The accipiters are also blessed with extremely long legs and impressively big feet on the end of them. Working at close quarters they need to be able to stick a leg out at strange angles to catch their prey. Sparrowhawks are definitively bird catchers and have very delicate feet, while the bigger goshawk is better equipped and females, in particular, can and will take large ground game.

Accipiters

This group of hawks are true woodland hunters and therefore are very quick over short distances. They are very brave and will tackle most suitable quarry. Crazy and psychotic, they test a falconer's patience and skill but at their best reward it fully. Their manic personalities make them prone to epileptiform fits and, to prevent these, they should be given thiamine (vitamin B12) on a regular basis. In training they will reach a hunting weight before they reach an obedient one, so obedience is a greater problem than entering them. A lot of social imprinting is done nowadays to produce a steadier, more amenable bird.

An unfortunate characteristic of this group is that their feathers are easily damaged, so they are often kept in a protective tail sheath to prevent this. Anyone flying an accipiter will become proficient at repairing (imping) broken feathers.

Cooper's Hawk (Accipiter cooperii)

A useful American bird midway between a goshawk and a sparrowhawk for size. Slightly steadier, and a little heavier built than its

The Finnish goshawk is one of the larger geographical sub-species of this traditional shortwing.

European cousins, the 'Coop' makes an ideal magpie/partridge/crow bird and will also take pheasant, small rabbit and squirrel. Not many are bred in UK so the price is high. Birds from the eastern states of the US are normally considered to be bigger than those from the west.

Goshawk (Accipiter gentilis)

Still regarded as the definitive hawk, the goshawk is a fast, moody and aggressive hunter. Usually flown from the fist, it will work well over dogs, particularly in heavy woodland. The females will readily take flying or ground game, while the males, with their long, slender toes, are rarely keen on rabbit. Gos-owning is a matter of time and dedication. They can be very expensive to buy, particularly as they can drop dead or fly off at any time. Size affects price and big Finnish females are most sought after, with Czech or German males being much more affordable.

In the UK goshawks suffer from their reputation as a difficult bird to train. This stems largely from T. H. White's book *The Goshawk*, in which he struggled with his hawk's wayward temperament. In fact this classic account is almost a textbook on how to make training a hawk as difficult as possible. Ever since then it seems British falconers have been over-emphasizing the goshawk's intractability and, by inference, their own superior skill as a falconer in successfully mastering it. Gos-flying has become the benchmark of excellence.

What a contrast this is to other European falconers. They happily lend their goshawks to friends and visitors, and will take them, often unhooded, into public places. In fact they seem to cope very easily with them. There is certainly a challenge in keeping them healthy, but an awful lot of goshawks seem perfectly unaware of their reputation.

Sparrowhawk (Accipiter nisus)

For its size this must be the most sporting of all hawks, and it is capable of taking quite large quarry. The male (musket) is too tiny to tackle anything above pigeon size (but then it

27

Harris hawks are gregarious and hunt in family groups in the wild.

probably weighs less than 150g/5oz itself), and its vulnerability to weight loss makes it difficult to fly, so females are preferred. It is an advantage to have them imprinted, as they will be obedient at a higher weight, and their screaming, which is quite tolerable, helps to locate them in dense cover. Sparrowhawks are hard to breed in captivity, as domestic violence is never very far away, so they are not readily available. They are definitely not suitable for beginners!

Like the larger goshawk, the sparrowhawk is ready to hunt a long time before it is obedient. This means that it has very little body weight in reserve by the time it is reliable enough to be taken out across the fields. Experienced sparrowhawk men are careful to give little buffer meals, and to carry glucose and/or fresh liver with them as a quick pick-me-up. Unless you can honestly say that you are consistent and careful in monitoring your bird's weight and condition, you should not consider a spar. Would-be spar flyers are recommended to try and find a copy of Jack Mavrogordato's book (sadly out of print) *A Hawk for the Bush*.

Harris Hawk (Parabuteo unicinctus)

Neither an accipiter nor a buzzard, the Harris is an amazing bird that can fly in a variety of styles and habitats. Harris hawks are the only gregarious bird of prey and are exceptionally tame and obedient, making them ideal for the serious falconer who cannot readily devote time to a bird on a daily basis. This species is easily the most frequently used hunting bird in the UK. The Harris hawk is capable of taking a wide range of flying and ground game. Youngsters are prone to screaming and should be avoided if you live in a very built-up area. Weights vary according to country of origin and some are called Superiors because of their greater stature. Females weigh from 850g–1.15kg (1lb 14oz–2lb 8oz), with males making 500–750g (1lb 2oz–1lb 10oz).

The Harris has revolutionized falconry. Not only has it made it possible for more people to practise the sport than before, it has also opened the door to social hawking. Because of their gregarious nature Harris hawks can be flown loose at the same time, even if they do not know each other. This means that friends can go out together without risk of their birds

Barn owl with young handler. A suitable starting point for children provided they have close supervision.

committing genocide. It has also made it possible for the complete novice to hunt with trained birds, opening up commercial hawking and popularizing the sport.

This has led some falconers to unfairly denigrate the Harris. The fact that virtually anyone can train and fly one with reasonable success does not make it a lesser performer. We are still finding out about this remarkable species and, as we get better at flying it, our admiration for it is growing. I have had the good fortune to visit Harry McElroy, the pioneer of Harris flying, in his desert home in Arizona. What a discovery he made, and what a debt we owe him for the pleasure the Harris has given.

Owls

The use of owls for hunting is something that comes up from time to time. It is possible but unrewarding. In the 1980s, when bird prices rocketed, several falconers attempted to hunt with owls and claimed some success but now that decent birds are affordable hardly anyone bothers with the owls any more.

The reason is that when a bird has been successful you have to remove its quarry from it. You can then continue on for further sport. The hawk releases its kill because you have 'made in' and covered its victim. This fools it into thinking that you have 'magicked' it away and, as there is no point in hanging on to something which has disappeared, the hawk steps off its kill for a more visible reward.

The owl depends more on touch and hearing and less on sight. Being unable to see its prize will not convince it that there is nothing there. And sitting in long, wet grass for a couple of hours trying to detach an eagle owl from an increasingly mangled rabbit ranks fairly low on my list of exciting things to do.

Many enthusiasts fly owls for pleasure, the barn owl (*Tyto alba*) being one of the commonest birds of prey in captivity. They make a good point of entry for children (who must have an involved adult for overall responsibility), as barn owls are usually very tame and easy to handle. All owls that are to be flown must be hand-reared to achieve any degree of tameness and obedience.

29

Kites, Vultures and Other Scavengers

Falconry and hawking is about catching live quarry. Enough said. Display givers do sometimes use these carrion eaters because they are very large and impressive.

IMPRINTING

Imprinting is the process whereby young creatures develop a species identity. Simply put, they adopt the first object they see, particularly if it rewards their attention with food. I once found an orphan lamb beside a fence. It thought it was a fence post. Even taken into the house the lamb would lie beside the table leg.

In birds of prey the youngsters (eyasses) quickly recognize their parents, and by the time they are fully fledged they have a fairly deep sense of what they are. Unfortunately they may be taken for training before they have become independent of their parents. Depriving them of food to make them responsive can then induce imprinting on their handler as a parent substitute.

Captive-bred birds of prey are often hatched in incubators and reared, to varying degrees, by hand. They are very likely to perceive themselves to be human, or, at least, identify you as a parent.

Disadvantages of Imprinting

In the nest young birds of prey grow extremely quickly. They achieve full size and independence in a time span that would be the equivalent of a human baby being full-grown and at work by the age of six months. Within weeks of hatching they are as big as their parents and blessed with the same armoury. Theirs is a competitive life: the first to 'mug' mum or dad gets the food. In consequence they attack their parents for food, simultaneously screaming at the top of their voices. A nest of young peregrines can be heard up to a mile away! Only once the youngsters have eventually become independent, following constructive and increasing neglect from their parents, do they shut up and ignore other members of their species.

In captivity, if the eyass identifies you as its parent, it will attack you for food and scream non-stop at the sight of you. You can bet your neighbours will really love you. Until you have trained it to return, and to be approached on a kill, it will not have the freedom to hunt for itself. Moreover, it will be fed whenever you call it back or pick it up from a kill or its lure. Do not, therefore, be surprised if its infantile behaviour persists for the rest of its life.

Not all imprinting is bad. Owls are a case in point, as are some of the smaller raptors such as sparrowhawks and merlins. In the first instance owls are imprinted to make them tame. Without this they will be difficult, if not impossible, to train. The reason for imprinting small, delicate hawks and falcons is that, being tamer, they can be flown in a higher condition, making them less vulnerable to sudden weight loss and more resilient to disease.

Hacking

In the past antisocial behaviour was circumvented by putting the young falcon out to hack. This amounted to a group of fledgling youngsters being allowed free-range from a safe and secure feeding station to which they would return each night. Being in a peer group they retained their self-image as birds, but had no older bird to bully for food. The food would be tied down in the 'hack site' while they were absent, so that no connection could be made between food and humans. As their flying and hunting skills developed they would eventually fail to return. This usually coincided with their first kill, a feat that would be unlikely to be repeated on a daily basis. The next time they returned to the 'hack site' they would be caught up to commence their training.

There is an accepted risk in this procedure, in that a very successful young bird may well kill on consecutive days, and may never need to return to base. As eyasses can no longer be taken from the wild for free, and as today's

Mantling over food. This jealous reaction is most common in imprinted birds.

world offers rather more dangers than in the past, very few falconers have the opportunity to practise hacking. One or two commercial breeders do, however, still offer hacked youngsters for sale.

Hand-Rearing

At its most extreme hand-rearing can consist of an incubator-hatched eyass being fed by hand from the very first day. It will see people as parents, and will scream (and scream) continuously. It will also exhibit serious aggression over food, perhaps striking at your face. Another product of such imprinting will be a deep suspicion of anyone near its food, making it difficult to pick up off a kill or a lure. Quite possibly it will develop the awkward habit of carrying kills to prevent you reaching them. Certainly it will mantle furiously at your approach, pressing its wings and tail so firmly against the ground, or your fist when being fed, that it will repeatedly break its major feathers. Such a bird is known as a **food imprint,** and frequently by less complimentary names.

Social Imprinting

This is a more sophisticated development whereby the eyass is raised in a human environment, without thinking of people as parents. This is achieved by keeping the eyass in a substitute nest, such as a basket or box, from which it can explore. From this secure nursery it will watch your comings and goings without fear. It can be picked up, carried about and generally played with. The more it is handled the tamer it will become. To prevent food imprinting it should be removed from its 'nest', while food is being placed there. When it is returned it will find the food for itself, thereby avoiding the need for parents. You will have a bird that is very tame but which does not exhibit the screaming and aggression of the **food imprint**. It will still mantle and carry, as it sees itself as a human and you, therefore, as a competitor.

A bird reared in this way will, however, be unlikely to relate to its own species and so will have no potential as breeding stock except through artificial insemination. This is quite inappropriate for the novice to consider.

European eagle owl calling for food. Mature birds hoot to their handler as a greeting.

Group or Creche Rearing

Where more than one eyass are reared in a **creche** together, they will be socially imprinted on humans but will also retain their self-image as a bird. They will have the same virtues and vices as the single social imprint but will be more likely to breed.

Older eyasses (almost fully fledged) can be taken from their parents, and then **group-reared in seclusion aviaries** (that is, ones with solid sides). They will be unable to imprint on humans, but will also lose their parent dependency so will exhibit markedly less noise and aggression over food. Once training commences they will be more self-sufficient than a parent-reared bird of the same age. This technique is often used with Harris hawks in an attempt to reduce the potential for screaming.

Imprinting Owls

Where this is to be done I would suggest that you leave the parents to do the feeding during the first two to three weeks. By then the youngsters will probably be pulling at their own food, or at least gulping down quite large pieces by themselves. Ideally several owlets should be reared simultaneously so that they retain their bird self-image. However, they can be reared in isolation without too many problems. Owls are not noisy imprints, in fact barn owls sound like minute, demented, steam engines, while the eagle owls seem to restrict their conversation to monosyllabic belches.

Aggression over food is rarely a problem with owls. This is because owls are seldom kept chronically hungry, as would be done with a hawk at hunting weight. They are fed on appetite, and their obedience stems from imprinting rather than genuine hunger. As they reach sexual maturity, they may well establish a relationship with one special person. They will remain 'soppy tame' with them but may well be aggressive to anyone seen as a potential rival.

It is worth getting as many different people as possible to handle a young owl. This will reduce the chance of it selecting one 'special friend'.

Imprinting Small Hawks and Falcons

The novice falconer is unlikely to start off with a small, delicate hawk or falcon, apart

32

from possibly the kestrel. Kestrels are charming birds, and because they are small enough for a child to handle, are sometimes recommended as a first bird for young falconers. I cannot stress enough that children should not be given a bird of prey unless they have an experienced and involved adult to supervise them on a daily (even hourly) basis. As a general rule the smaller the bird, the more difficult it is to keep it in good condition or at a correct weight. The parameters are too tight. It usually ends in tears, with the bird being either lost or dead.

This is why we imprint kestrels, merlins, sparrowhawks and other small raptors. Being tamer there is less need for strict weight control, so the bird is stronger and more resilient to illness. Happily the noise problem is not as bad as with the bigger falcons. Indeed imprinted sparrowhawks have an attractive, plaintive call, which is a great help if you are trying to find one in thick woodland. Aggression over food can be very evident but, of course, the bird is unable to do any serious damage.

Creative Variations on Imprinting

I know of two examples of enterprising and creative imprinting. One we did ourselves with a pair of baby sparrowhawks that were being raised specifically for a filming project. We kept them in a gravel-filled bath in a corner of our workshop. This was open to the public and a daily succession of tourists filed through, invariably stopping to play with them. On the side of the bath the inventor of this technique, Richard Smith, fixed a mount on which an old falconry glove could be slotted. Within the circle of the thumb and fingers he placed a shallow dish. Whenever we wanted to feed the youngsters, we would have them removed by helpful visitors, while food was placed in the dish. With the glove securely fastened to the 'nest', the youngsters would be brought back in. Immediately they would throw themselves bodily at the glove.

By the time they were ready to start training they were completely food-imprinted on the glove. They showed no aggression towards people or the bare hand. Neither did they mantle over their food on the fist, but they would come like a rocket to the glove from any distance, even with a crop full of food.

The second example was a technique developed by Ronnie Forbes with a very young ferruginous buzzard. Now anyone who knows these birds will shudder at the thought of an imprinted one. They are large and enjoy a reputation for being pretty aggressive without needing any extra help. However, Ronnie intended to hunt in the Grampian Mountains, where the bird could get a lot of lift and could literally see for miles.

He placed the young hawk in a seclusion aviary, so that the bird could not see him or anything else. Food was to be put into the aviary via a tube, as even the sight of his hand could not be permitted. At food times he would blow an 'Acme Thunderer' referee's whistle, while he approached the aviary (there is no record of his neighbours' reaction to this method!). The bird learnt to associate this noise with food and became imprinted on it. Once training started it would return promptly to the fist in response to the whistle. As he said himself, 'She'll go up like a skylark, and hunt up to a mile and a half ahead of me, but she's totally obedient to the whistle.'

This was put to the test at a field meeting one day. It was Ronnie's slip and he released his bird to chase a blue hare. Unfortunately a goshawk got loose at the same time and was quickly overtaking the ferruginous. There was no doubt that it would be the first to get to the quarry, and few doubts as to the outcome when the ferruginous arrived moments later. With great presence of mind Ronnie blew his 'Thunderer'. To everyone's amazement including, I suspect, Ronnie's, the ferruginous turned in mid-air and came back to his fist.

On the same day Ronnie got the bird back in the middle of a plantation after it had gone on the soar and was way out of sight. This imprinting did not stop the bird being aggressive towards its handler, but no more than any average ferruginous might have been.

Exceptions to Imprinting Rules

Imprinting is not a black and white situation as so much depends on the type and extent of imprinting, and one of the main variables is the bird itself. Two examples from my own experience should serve to illustrate this.

A falcon breeder from whom I was buying a bird threw in a two-week-old kestrel as a 'luck penny'. 'Take it,' he explained, 'It's a third-round youngster and was the only egg in the clutch. The parents kill their young so I always creche-rear them. This is the last chick of the year and I have nothing else to rear it with.'

The kestrel chick was allowed complete freedom to grow up in our workshop. It fouled all over the sales goods and, on one occasion, managed to ring up over £8,000 on the cash register. We all played with it and, regretfully, fed it by hand. It should have been the worst-mannered, screaming food-imprint in the world. But it hadn't read the books. It never screamed, never showed aggression and never mantled over food. It was, however, very obedient and a super flier. Oddly, as it fledged, its feathers came out in mature, male plumage.

The second example worked the other way. I trained a 7-month-old female, parent-reared Harris hawk, which had lived among a peer group in an aviary for the last three months. At the start of the hunting season I caught her up. It took four days to get her to jump to the glove and, on that same day, I entered her to game. She was completely unmanned, had never worked on a creance, and had only been fed on the glove briefly that morning. For the next two months she killed every day, often several times. She was always allowed to end her day on a kill, from which she ate her ration.

After two months she suddenly began screaming at me. Within a few days of this she managed to foot me around the eyes, a practice she would repeat, given the chance. Strangely she only does this around her perch or in the mews. She has also killed another Harris on its perch. Out hunting she is beautifully mannered, working well with the dogs and ferrets, and will amiably share kills with other birds.

How did such psychotic, imprinted behaviour arise in a bird that had been brought up in the optimum circumstances? At least it shows we are never too old to learn. Do you remember when I said that there is no such thing as an expert falconer?

ACQUIRING A BIRD OF PREY

In Britain it is illegal to take a bird of prey from the wild. Only falconry centres, zoos and private collections that have zoo licences, are able to import wild-taken stock, and must prove a conservation case for doing so. Injured wild birds may enter the system when their injuries are such that it is thought unrealistic to re-release them. However, where injuries make them unlikely to fly properly, euthanasia is normally seen as the best option, except for rarer species that have breeding value.

This means that all hawks, as far as the beginner is concerned, are captive-bred. The various journals and bird magazines offer a wide selection for sale. Unfortunately there are some unscrupulous breeders who produce poor-quality stock. The novice must get training before buying a bird, so I would recommend that they ask their instructor's advice. Alternatively your local club will steer you towards recommended breeders in your area. Take a knowledgeable person with you when you go to collect your bird.

CHAPTER 3

Preparing for the New Hawk

HOUSING

The most important thing to remember about birds of prey is that they can fly much better than you do – and the direction is often away from you!

For this reason, and it should be ingrained in the memory of every aspiring falconer, you must always be security conscious. The days when hawks and falcons were regularly stolen are long gone, so our concern is less to prevent theft than to ensure that the bird is unable to escape. Equally it needs to be protected from attack by dogs, cats, foxes, stoats, ferrets (!), other raptors, and from the worst of the elements.

For every person who builds a luxury, designer pad for their hawk, there will be another who will convert existing buildings for the purpose. Your bird will need the following:

- A secure place to be kept at night.
- A safe area for the daytime.
- A secure travelling box/cadge.
- A cheap and portable/disposable, temporary, overnight perch.

Overnight Accommodation

What accommodation to prepare depends on your existing resources and the type of hawk you are going to get. Space is not a major issue as the roosting bird does not fly or move about much, but you should ensure that a bating hawk (that is, one that is thrashing about in a panic or temper) has sufficient space that it cannot injure itself. Circulation of air and allowing enough space for its droppings, which with the larger hawks can be impressively widespread, are much more serious considerations.

If space is limited it may be hard to sacrifice a whole shed or outbuilding to the hawk. A **portable perching arrangement** can be used, which can be tucked away during the day, allowing the building to revert to its original purpose. This also applies when you are away from home and using other people's buildings. I have successfully used board perches, free-standing bow perches and modified screen perches. I would not recommend the technique adopted by my son on one occasion, however. Lacking a suitable aviary he simply released a pair of merlins in his bedroom, where they coexisted very happily with him. Possibly only a teenage boy's room could have survived this without the evidence of their occupation being remarked amidst the general squalor!

Modifying an Existing Building

You may be able to designate a shed or outbuilding as a permanent mews for your hawk. This would allow you to keep it 'free lofted' (untied and able to move about). Such an arrangement is preferable, as any extra exercise will be beneficial (but remember the roosting hawk does not move much).

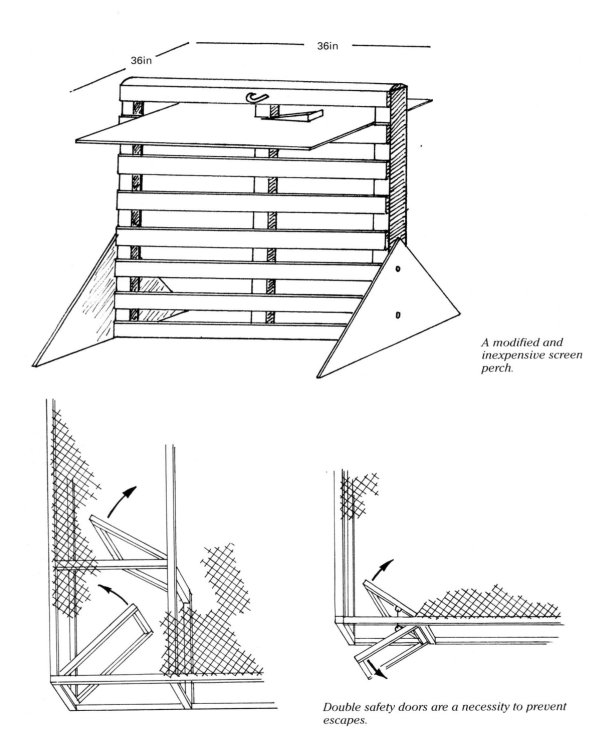

A modified and inexpensive screen perch.

Double safety doors are a necessity to prevent escapes.

Doors

Once again remember that birds of prey can fly much better than you do – and usually away from you!

If you keep a hawk loose, in a building or aviary, there is a very real risk that it might get out as you go in or leave. Some kind of 'airlock' or double door system is essential. Another possibility is to use the lower half of a stable door, as hawks tend to fly up rather than down and are unlikely to escape as you enter.

Windows

Most existing buildings will have a window, which offers another possible escape route. The hawk will benefit from freely circulating air, so leave windows open. For security you can permanently fasten dowelling or thick bamboo rods vertically to the inside of the window frame. These should be so rigid and close together that the bird cannot force its

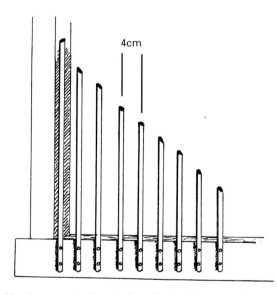

4cm

Hawks cannot cling to dowelled windows so there is less likelihood of damage to tail feathers.

way between them. Because it is vertical the dowelling is not attractive to the hawk as a perch, and any attempt to cling to it simply results in the hawk sliding gracefully down. Its tail may project between the bars but there will be no major damage to it. Never use mesh on windows as the bird will cling to it and damage its tail feathers.

I once kept a male Harris in a converted building that had a large window overlooking our yard. The glass had been taken out and thick bamboo canes had been securely screwed, vertically, to the frame. They were about 4cm (1.5in) apart and the window measured about 1m (3ft) from top to bottom. One day I heard my son shouting for help and rushed out to see what was the matter. He had been walking past carrying his sparrowhawk when my Harris had shot straight through the bars of the window to attack the smaller bird (the hatred Harris hawks have for goshawks seems to apply to sparrowhawks as well). There must have been some delay, as my son had had sufficient time to shield his bird from mine. When I got to him he was waltzing round in circles, trying to keep his back between the two birds.

Even knowing that the hawk had got through the bars we still found it difficult to believe. There was no obvious gap and we could only guess that the Harris had used its body as a wedge, to spring the bars far enough apart for it to get through. I was reluctant to put a strengthening bar across the centre of the window, as this would have offered it a perch of sorts. Instead we reduced the overall span of the bamboo canes by boarding off a section at the top, and fastening the canes again at a lower point on this board.

Walls

Check thoroughly for any protruding nails or screws, and remove anything that offers a semblance of a perch. A hawk will try to use the tiniest toehold at times and will damage its feathers in the attempt. Hang plastic sheeting where the hawk will mute (excrete).

Floors

Concrete or tiled bases may be mopped clean, and vinolay or some similar floor covering can be used on wooden floors. Cover with white wood shavings, *not* sawdust, hay, straw, peat or sharp sand. Fine dust can affect the bird's respiratory system. Remove soiled shavings regularly, and change the floor covering completely every two or three weeks. Fungal infections from mouldy bedding can be fatal. If you are using a portable perch it is a good idea to put down a base of flattened, cardboard boxes and cover them with newspaper. You can then change this top layer daily and simply replace the cardboard at the end of each week.

Make sure that the floor of your building, if it is a wooden sectional one, clears the ground by at least 15 cm (6in). Any less and it will attract rats, which like to be able to touch their backs against the roof of their tunnels.

Ceilings

Make sure that the ceiling is not so high that you are unable to reach a hawk that is roosting in the rafters. If you use any sort of mesh to make a false ceiling make sure it is rigid, and of a size that will not trap a bird's legs or head. Any mesh used must be of plastic or plastic-coated material. Avoid chicken wire, which will quickly decimate your bird's plumage (and also damage its cere), and chain link, in which your hawk can catch and damage its legs.

Perches

Place no more than three perches well apart to encourage flight. For hawks, buteos and owls use natural branches set horizontally, and remove all side branches and twigs. Suspend the one that offers the hawk the best view to create a **swing perch**. The bird will have to use extra muscles to balance itself, both on landing and when taking off.

Falcons like flat surfaces to perch on and you should supply isolated shelves for them. Make these semicircular to minimize damage

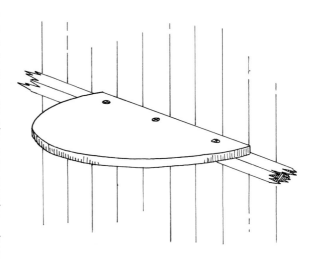

A semicircular falcon perch reduces wear on the tail feathers.

to tail feathers. Astroturf gives a kinder surface to these perches and can also be removed and cleaned.

Safe Daytime Area

Most days a hawk will be put out in the open to 'weather', that is, be exposed to fresh air, sun, wind and rain. The risks are:

- Equipment failure, when jesses, swivel, leash or perch component break.
- Falconer failure, tying an insecure or faulty knot.
- Attack by dogs, foxes, cats, ferrets, other raptors.
- Extreme weather.

The only safe provision is a totally enclosed, properly constructed weathering. This should resemble an open-fronted bicycle shed, with solid walls at the back and sides and a secure, rigid, mesh screen at the front. The mesh should be pretty small to prevent entry by

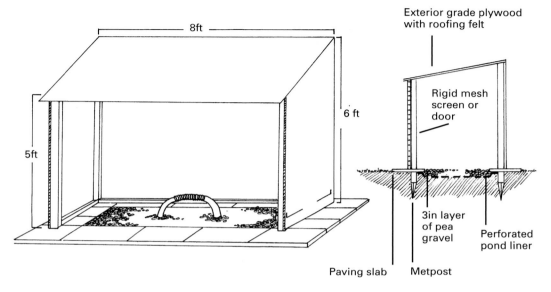

Design for a secure weathering area.

ferrets, stoats, mink or wild polecats. I have had a hawk killed on its perch by an escaped ferret.

The overall dimensions should be sufficient to permit the hawk or falcon to extend its wings without damaging them when at the furthest point of its leash.

The floor should be covered with pea gravel or aggregate to provide a well-drained surface. You may install a plastic sheet underneath this to prevent weeds coming up, but allow some drainage holes. Clean the gravel by hosing and raking it.

I once made the mistake of leaving a kestrel out in what I regarded as a secure weathering. The weather was warm and I was confident that it was safe. The next day there were only its feet, still in their jesses, tied to the perch. A fox had dug under the side walls to get to it. This sad lesson taught me to sink wire netting into the ground, to a depth of about 45cm

(18in). Alternatively you can simply lay paving stones around the perimeter so that foxes at least have a long way to dig.

An arrangement I like is suitable for eagles and eagle owls, where the bird's safety is not really an issue. It consists of two very large and heavy logs with a taut, steel wire stretched between them. One log is within a conventional but open-fronted weathering. A chain, acting as a leash and fastened to the swivel, runs along the steel line, giving the bird ample opportunity to fly from log to log.

A Purpose-Built Aviary

An aviary combines both a mews and weathering, and is the recommended accommodation for birds of prey. It must have:

• Sheltered and roofed zones.
• A minimum size of twice the wingspan wide and three times the wingspan long.

39

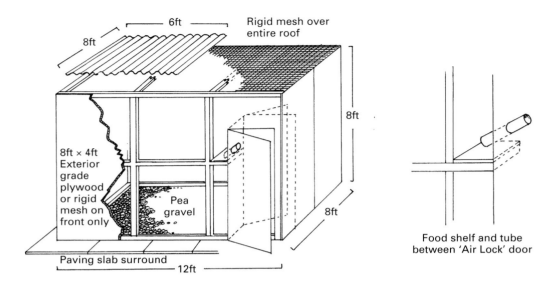

Design for an aviary, an essential facility for breeding and moulting birds.

- Non-abrasive, rigid and preferably plastic-coated mesh.
- Easily cleaned and weed-free floor.
- Base of walls to be tunnel-proof.
- Double 'air lock' door.

Base

Dig this out to a shallow depth of perhaps 10cm (4in). Line it with plastic sheeting (pond liner or builder's sheeting) which you should puncture at intervals to allow drainage. Then fill the base with pea gravel or aggregate. Place paving slabs all around the edge so that you have a 60cm (2ft)-wide surround. This will act as a base for your walls and will deter foxes. Paving stones sunk vertically would have the same effect and use less space but are much harder work.

Walls

These may be of mesh or solid construction. It is advisable, for ease of replacement, to make them in framed sections or to use very rigid sheets of mesh or board. These can be fastened to a framework of supporting cross-members which link stout wooden uprights. The uprights may be set in concrete or fixed with 'Metposts'.

There are good heavy-duty, rigid, nylon meshes available on the market today (look at aviary netting under www.knowlenets.co.uk). Alternatively use a galvanized mesh like Weldmesh or Twilweld. Materials to avoid are chain link (full of nasty twists to tear talons out), chicken wire (you might as well take a chainsaw to your bird's feathers) or lightweight nylon mesh (if very light it may tear, and it will eventually go brittle in sunlight and disintegrate).

An outer layer of chicken wire at a lower level is recommended to deter entry by ferrets, and by small creatures like mice, rats and frogs. These last, while not posing a threat to your hawk's safety, can ruin your plans for hawking. More than one falconer has gone to take his bird from its aviary only to discover it has already eaten.

You may opt to install solid panels instead of mesh. Interwoven fence panels were very popular but because they are made of such

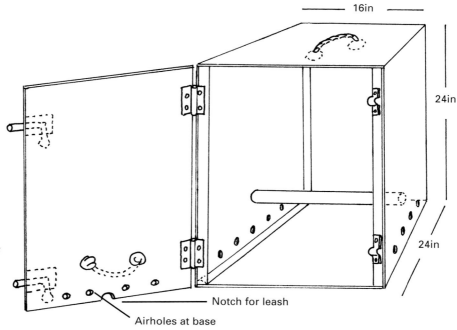

— 16in —

24in

24in

Travelling boxes are also useful for overnight accommodation and as emergency hospital cages.

Notch for leash

Airholes at base

thin slats of wood they become very brittle and fragile. It is better to use exterior grade plywood sheeting of the weight used by builders to form concrete. Annual treatment with pet-friendly preservative is essential to stop damp rot and fungus, which can provide a perfect breeding ground for the deadly respiratory infection aspergillosis.

The advantages of having mesh sides to an aviary are that they allow you to watch the bird, and the bird to have mental stimulus. Air can circulate freely, which reduces the likelihood of fungus or mould building up. However, accipiters are usually too nervous and highly strung to relax in an open aviary, while the falcons, which are not equipped to fly in tight circles, are prone to crash into the mesh. For most birds of prey it is advisable to have solid-sided aviaries, particularly if you wish to try breeding them.

Your aviary design should provide sheltered areas whatever the wind strength or direction. Unlike its wild cousin, the captive bird of prey

does not have a limitless choice of perches, so it must always be able to get out of the worst of the weather.

Travelling Box
A travelling box must have:

- Easily cleaned, solid and light-proof sides, top and bottom.
- A suitable perch at an appropriate height.
- Sufficient room to avoid feather damage.
- Air holes below line of sight.
- Secure door with place for leash to be passed through.
- Strong carrying and anchoring points.

Travelling boxes are invaluable for a buteo or accipiter because they prevent it fouling all over your car. The bird will be calm because it is effectively inside a hood, so will arrive fresh and relaxed. Also, when you are away from home, the travelling box can double as secure overnight accommodation.

A cadge was the four-wheel-drive vehicle of its day and is still invaluable.

Cadge

A cadge must have:

- Solid, stable construction.
- Well-padded perching places of suitable width.
- Good anchoring points

Cadges are useful for hooded falcons and several can travel on the same cadge. On arriving it is simple to step inside the cadge, and carry the whole team of falcons for as far and as long as you wish. I never used a cadge until I took part in a historical pageant, portraying 150 years of field sports, and was asked to supply one. I have used one every day since.

Hygiene

- Regularly scrub all surfaces with a rotation of bleach and specialist raptor disinfectants (such as Virkon) and antibacterial agents, in the recommended-strength solution. Unless specifically told to leave a cleansing agent untouched, rinse off very thoroughly.
- Change branch perches frequently, every three or four months.
- Remove soiled shavings and surplus food/pellets from internal floors on a daily basis.

> ### Car Safety for Falcons
>
> Do not use swinging air fresheners in your car. They kill.
> Do not leave birds of prey in closed vehicles in warm weather. They can cook, just like dogs.

- Paint concrete, stone or brick buildings annually with emulsion or whitewash.
- Treat wooden buildings annually with creosote or pet-friendly wood preservative.

EQUIPMENT

Get all your equipment (properly called furniture) before buying your bird. Start with a **chest freezer** for storing bird food; spouses tend to have a strange aversion to the family's food sharing freezer space with dead rats, chicks, and so on. On the subject of food, you should also get a **vitamin supplement** that is designed specifically for raptors. Then, working from the bird downwards, as it were, you will need the following.

Jesses

You will need a pair of leather jesses, one jess for each leg. Nowadays everyone fits true or false aylmeri anklets, with button jesses. Any reputable equipment maker will use kangaroo or calf hide for these. Specify the sex and species of your intended hawk when buying them. I prefer the false aylmeri anklets, which are easier to fit and remove. Make sure they are well-oiled and supple. You will need two pairs of jesses: a pair of mews jesses to fasten the bird with when not flying, and a pair of hunting jesses for when it is free.

With falcons, and those owls which are also to be kept on block perches, you should ensure that the jesses are sufficiently short that your bird is unlikely to straddle the block, which is a sure recipe for feather damage. With small birds this is often inconvenient, as the jesses are then so short that they are hard to hold on

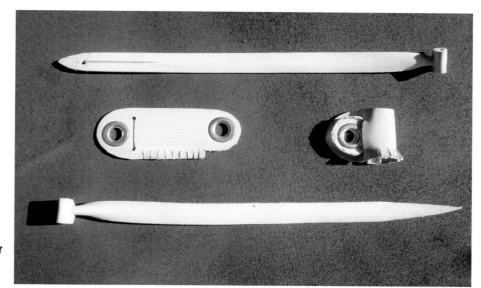

False aylmeri anklets and button jesses are the most sensible and popular system.

A bird with jesses that are too long, or on a block that is too small, can end up damaging its feathers if it straddles its perch.

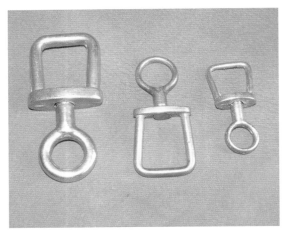

Swivels are a small but vital piece of equipment. These are cast from bronze and stainless steel.

to properly. Using a bigger perch solves that problem but creates two others: because the perch is now larger than the bird needs it will get covered in the bird's faeces, and the falcon's tail will also rub against the block.

Swivels

These link the jesses to the leash and prevent either getting twisted up around the hawk's legs. Get two as they can easily be dropped and lost. Swivels come in a variety of designs, but avoid any that are riveted or welded – they should be solid cast. The larger part of the swivel should be square to prevent the jesses working down over it. If that happens the swivel will no longer be able to rotate freely, thus causing the jesses to twist.

Leash

Again, it makes sense to get two, made of firm, flat or round, braided nylon. The knotted end must be heat-sealed, with a leather washer against it to prevent wear.

The falconer's knot has been known to come loose under the attentions of persistent hawks. It is not always correctly tied and can result in a hawk escaping with its leash trailing behind it. To avoid this knot I recommend using a **loop leash**, fastened with

the button through the swivel. I do not recommend those blocks that have a second, smaller ring welded on to the existing larger ring for the loop leash. I have had this weld fractured by a kestrel, which flew off with a quite a heavy hoop of metal dangling from its leash. Very luckily it got snagged on a television aerial and I was able to recover it, but it taught me to mistrust over-complicated equipment. Nowadays I stick to the simplest designs and 'let who will be clever'.

Both the falconer's knot and the loop leash are covered in Chapter 5.

Gauntlet

Although a welding glove is adequate for small birds you will want a proper falconry glove. Most falconers get too heavy a glove for their first bird, so it is sensible to ask your instructor what you need. Tassels are a complete nuisance – they get in the way and advertise that you are a novice. A glove should have a metal ring built in, to which your hawk may be tied when being carried.

Cleaning gloves is a problem as they soon get dirty with blood and so on sticking to them. Scraping dirt off them with a knife is fine in the short term but you will eventually have to clean them more thoroughly. Some leathers (buckskin for example) retain their softness despite being washed. Others go hard as they dry. With the latter I always rinse them in warm water, on which I have first floated a layer of leather-dressing oil, like neatsfoot oil or Hydrophane. The leather takes this up and is soon supple again, once it has dried and been used.

Hood

A hood is essential for falcons and useful for all birds of prey. A lot of hoods are beautifully made and expensive but fit badly. Human hat sizes go in one-eighths of an inch, with different fittings for round and long heads, so think how slight a variation will make a hood uncomfortable for a bird. Ideally have several

There are various hood styles but a good fit is the only important criterion.

Bewit

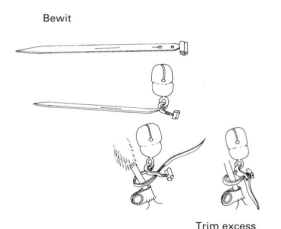

Trim excess

Bells should be fastened to the hawk's leg with a leather bewit.

hoods available to try. I recently made a hood for a new falcon that fitted perfectly first time, but on another occasion it was the thirty-second prototype that finally satisfied us both! There are different styles of hood.

Bells

Bells help you locate birds in cover and are necessarily made of brittle metal, which is why they ring. Every time the clapper hits the outside casing it beats it a little bit harder and thinner. The bell sounds best just before it cracks. Treat bells as disposables; the most expensive bell is unlikely to last any longer than the cheapest. For the novice, stick to fastening them on the leg, rather than a tail-mount, and use a leather bewit (small strap fastening the bell to the leg). The only time you can use a cable tie for fastening bells is when they are fixed directly to the anklet.

Telemetry

This is a must for falcons and advisable for every bird of prey. Where expense is an issue you can sometimes get just a transmitter (the cheaper part), that is compatible with a friend's receiver. If you do this you must check regularly that it is working, and be prepared to replace the batteries with careless abandon. Keep a written note of the receiver settings in your hawking bag. As telemetry is getting cheaper and better every year, you may be able

45

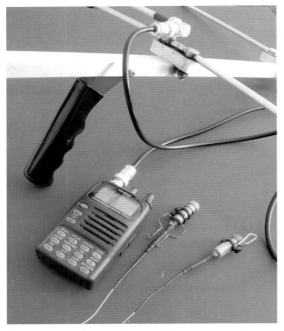

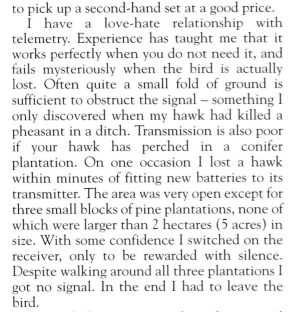

Telemetry receiver and transmitters are a major modern addition for the falconer.

Transmitter clipped on a falcon's leg bell.

to pick up a second-hand set at a good price.

I have a love-hate relationship with telemetry. Experience has taught me that it works perfectly when you do not need it, and fails mysteriously when the bird is actually lost. Often quite a small fold of ground is sufficient to obstruct the signal – something I only discovered when my hawk had killed a pheasant in a ditch. Transmission is also poor if your hawk has perched in a conifer plantation. On one occasion I lost a hawk within minutes of fitting new batteries to its transmitter. The area was very open except for three small blocks of pine plantations, none of which were larger than 2 hectares (5 acres) in size. With some confidence I switched on the receiver, only to be rewarded with silence. Despite walking around all three plantations I got no signal. In the end I had to leave the bird.

I passed the spot every day, often several times, and always got out the telemetry. Not a peep emerged from the blasted machine and I

became convinced that the cap had come off the transmitter, that the aerial had become detached or that some other disaster had befallen it. After ten days the local farmer's daughter, out riding her pony, came across the hawk on a kill. She telephoned me immediately and told me exactly where the bird was. I arrived within ten minutes only to find that the hawk had moved. However, I heard its bell and found it, still on its carcass, some 10m inside the plantation. Having recovered it I returned to my car. Out of interest, although I knew the telemetry batteries only claimed a six-day life span, I checked my receiver. I was rewarded with a steady 'bleep, bleep, bleep'. The wretched thing had been transmitting all the time, yet had failed to give a signal through the dense pines.

In fairness I have also recovered falcons that had gone several kilometres, including one that traversed the whole of Birmingham. On another occasion my signal was drowned

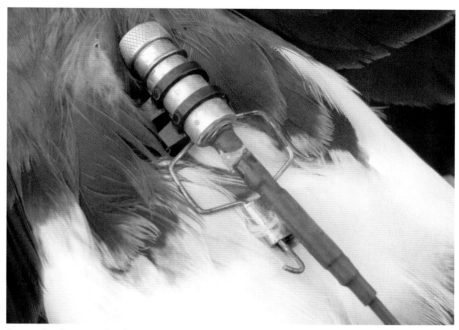

Transmitter on hunting hawk's tail mount, where it is least likely to get in the way.

out by a local radio cab firm, which was operating illegally on the same frequency.

Telemetry can be fastened to the hawk by a tail mount or on to a leg. Both methods present problems. Tail-mounted transmitters are fine on falcons, as they will not be damaged by the falcon struggling with its kill and are unlikely to be caught against anything while the bird is airborne. For hawks, however, there is a likelihood that the transmitter will snag on undergrowth or fences, not only risking damage to the equipment but, sometimes resulting in the deck feathers (the two central tail feathers) being ripped out. You then have to track down the transmitter.

I fasten transmitters on to my falcons' bells with a fishing snap tackle. This means that I can take them on and off very easily. My hunting hawks I fit with a very simple tail mount, a brass tube, with a thin suede lining glued in, that is in turn, glued to one of the deck feathers. That way at least I only lose one tail feather at a time!

Even this method has an unexpected danger. My son had put his female Harris hawk

into an aviary to moult, leaving the tail mount tube still fixed to her deck feather. He was confident that this would drop during the course of her moult, when he could either salvage the tube for reuse or simply fit a new one. One day, while preening herself, she got the hook of her beak stuck in the tail mount. When he found her she had fallen off her perch and into her bath, and had drowned. I have since heard of this happening to someone else's bird, so this is not an isolated incident.

Something like this accident could happen to any bird wearing a tail mount, whether it was on its perch or being free-lofted. However, you cannot take a tail mount off on a daily basis.

Hawking Bag

Any bag that can hold a lure, creance and food will suffice for the falcon flyer, but, if you intend hunting with your bird, the serious falconer (called an austringer if he flies a hawk) will need somewhere to stow the game as well. I use a **hawking waistcoat** (a cross between a waistcoat and a rucksack) as I find that a well-laden shoulder bag makes my spine

The creance line is wound around the stick in a figure of eight to avoid tangles.

twist. Both are available from equipment suppliers.

Do check your bag has been cleared of all food before it is hung up. Every falconer knows what it's like to find a small maggot factory has set up in his absence!

Creance

Your best friend and worst enemy, the creance comprises 30–40m (90–120ft) of strong, light, braided nylon line on a turned wooden handle. Do not economize on this by using any old twine or string. While the bird is tied securely to the creance you can safely test its obedience over a distance. However, you and the bird can become dependent on it. The longer you rely on the creance, the more your bird is learning to rely on you.

The worst job in falconry is winding it up (figure of eight style to prevent knots), so it is always a relief when your new bird is flying free and you can dispense with it. Before re-training your hawk at the start of the next season, do test the creance line for strength. It may have been subject to attack by mice or insects in the intervening time.

Lure

Designed to simulate your birds intended quarry, a lure may be swung as an imitation

bird or dragged as a dummy rabbit. As with all equipment, keep it simple and avoid over-ornate designs. It is the movement that will attract your bird, not the artistic merit. Of course the best lure is an actual carcass of the intended prey species, as it will look just like the real thing.

Perch

This must provide the sort of surface the bird would prefer in the wild. Falcons, coming from treeless areas, are designed to perch on rocks, and will want a flat surface to sit on. They will need a block. The tree-dwelling buteos, hawks and eagles want to get their feet around a branch, so you should furnish them with a bow perch. Owls may need either, according to the perching habits of the individual species. Both blocks and bows can be spiked for sticking in the ground, or free-standing for use on solid floors or in the car. The surface of any perch must be slightly irregular (a totally smooth surface will create pressure sores that in turn may allow entry to infection), and easily cleaned. Blocks can be topped with cork, Astroturf, carpet, wood or even concrete. Bows are bound with suede, rope or Astroturf.

Blocks should be just wide enough for the falcon to stand on comfortably; too narrow and

Ground and swung lures are used to attract the bird from a distance. It is the movement rather than being life-like that is important.

the bird must stand on its own toes, too wide and the tail cannot hang clear of the block.

From choice all hawks like to be high up. Perches have been produced that are perhaps 1m (3ft) or more high. Jumping up to them from the ground gives the hawk good exercise but, if it tries to fly off, it can build up a bit of speed before the long leash jolts it to a halt.

The solution to this is to fasten a length of elastic or rubber across a loop in the leash. This softens the impact as the leash straightens out and is kinder to the hawk's legs. Obviously the elastic or rubber can perish or snap, leaving the hawk's legs at risk again. Novices should avoid over-complications and stick to basic, simple equipment.

Both blocks and bow perches can have spikes to stick in the lawn or be free-standing for concrete surfaces or in the car.

Scales and record cards are used every day by the responsible falconer.

Scales

The old balance scales, with a range of weights, are less used now since many a bating hawk has scattered small weights across the floor. Most falconers use modified electronic scales which can be purchased from equipment suppliers. Always keep a written record of your bird's daily weight and performance alongside your scales. This is an essential part of your hawk management and will also provide a pleasant history to look back on in the future.

Bath

Any shallow (7–10cm/3–4in deep), plastic, gravel tray can be got from the local garden centre, and is suitable for most of the smaller birds of prey (up to 1kg/2lb weight). Beyond this you will need to buy a larger fibreglass, bird bath from falconry suppliers.

Stick

This is a surprisingly essential piece of equipment, used for tethering dog (and bird in emergencies), helping you over rough ground, streams, and for holding down barbed wire and electric fences. Also a stick is handy for beating cover. Ideally your stick should have a 'handle' of some sort, to use as a hook for dragging the bird, plus its kill, from bramble thickets or down from trees. It can also serve as a lofting pole, raising your bird up high for a slip on flat ground. Just cut one from the hedge as they always get lost or left behind.

First-Aid Kit

This is for you and the bird, and should include wound dressing powder/spray, plasters, vet's phone number and, if flying an accipiter, a made-up glucose solution with a syringe and tube for crop-tubing it into the bird (*see* Chapter 4).

Tool Kit

Although you should buy your initial equipment from reputable suppliers, you may want to make your own items from time to time. There are also a number of regular maintenance tasks that will need doing. Tools will include a sharp craft knife, long-nosed pliers, multi-hole punch pliers, eyelet fixing kits and tools, a steel straight edge/ruler, impact adhesive, saddler's point, needles and nylon thread and a set of key files for trimming your bird's beak (coping). You should also include a supply of good-quality calfskin or kangaroo hide for making fresh jesses.

Equipment Suppliers

Details of UK equipment (furniture) suppliers can be obtained from the IBR Falconry Directory at www.ibr.org.uk or, in the USA, from the Northwoods catalogue at www.northwoods.com.

CHAPTER 4

Day-to-Day Management

Keeping any livestock involves carrying out regular tasks to maintain the creature you are caring for in good health. Some, like feeding and cleaning, are daily concerns, others may require routine attention less frequently, perhaps on a weekly or monthly rota, while others may be quarterly or even annual duties. There will also be things to be done that are not predictable by your diary or calendar but are so likely to occur that they can be considered to be randomly routine.

Falconry has as many of these as any other animal-orientated activity. They all eat into the time you have available for your hawk, just as much as exercising and hunting it will do. Allow for them when setting up your original falconry 'budget' of time, cost and emotional resources.

By and large birds of prey are pretty healthy and resilient creatures. Kept in clean, adequate accommodation and fed wholesome food, they should thrive in your care, and reward this by flying and hunting well for you. This foundation, built on your husbandry skills, is the basis of your hawk's ongoing good health.

You have already prepared the weathering, mews, aviary or overnight facilities before getting your bird. Now is the time to look at the day-to-day management.

FEEDING

All birds of prey are carnivorous and are predators. They are nature's quality controllers, and in the wild eat their victims. This includes not just the muscle meat, but fur or feathers, the organs, skin and any small bones they can swallow. The closer we can keep to this diet in captivity the more likely they are to enjoy good, robust health. This is all the more important as the captive raptor is on a restricted ration and does not have the bodily reserves of its wild cousin. Therefore we should try to supply small carcasses, or parts of bigger ones, to satisfy the hawk's needs.

Muscle meat provides protein and some fat, while the organs, skin and bone supply the vitamin and mineral elements that are needed. When first eaten this is held in the crop, which is basically a skin bag in the bird's neck, in which initial digestion takes place. Ideally this needs cleaning on a daily basis. To achieve this the hawk forms a pellet out of its victim's fur or feather (which are known as castings), which acts as a scouring pad.

Tearing the carcass apart, particularly when stripping bones of every vestige of meat and sinew, should help the hawk keep its beak trimmed, and at the same time gives the resting hawk some pretty good exercise.

From this it is apparent that hawks should not be fed on butcher's meat or some kind of tinned preparation. Although the former can be used in the short term, this should always be considered as an emergency measure (perhaps if your freezer has suffered a terminal illness and your supply of hawk food has gone off). Should this occur the hawk will survive perfectly well for several days, or even longer periods, without having castings. However, these should be given regularly. If you are feeding butcher's meat then you can add dog or cat hair, small wisps of cotton wool, or even shredded wool as a substitute for fur. In his wonderful book *The Lure of the Falcon*, Gerald Summers recounts how his kestrel, a prisoner of war like himself, survived for some weeks on tinned salmon and bully beef. When she was eventually given a mouse to eat, she produced a perfectly normal pellet the next day.

Food Temperature

In the wild, raptors eat freshly killed quarry or carrion that is likely to be at the ambient temperature, which covers quite a wide range. We are told not to feed chilled or frozen food. This is good advice but do not panic if your bird does get hold of something colder, as it will probably cope perfectly well. Young birds of prey will pick at the chilled remnants of yesterday's meal until their parents bring a fresh, warm kill to the nest.

A golden eagle that had been lost for several hours (an easy thing to do in the Scottish mountains) was finally located on the frozen gralloch (tripes) of a red deer. It had been chiselling away with its great beak, and had a bulging crop that rattled when it was touched. One possibility was to 'milk' the crop (described later in this chapter), but this is an unpleasant process and the bird needs to be physically held, so is not a thing you can do easily with a large eagle. The eagle's owner opted to get the bird home as quickly as he could in order to get help to hold the eagle. This was a problem in itself, as the bird was a truculent and aggressive individual – a fact that was well known to anyone he could approach for assistance. As it happened the need never arose. With the warmth of the car, combined with the bird's own body heat, the contents of the crop had thawed before he got home. The eagle suffered no discomfort at all.

Sometimes a hawk will get hold of cooked meats. A kestrel of mine got lost once and was

rescued by a well-meaning member of the public. Unfortunately he fed the bird on sausage (it must have been starving to have eaten it) which nearly killed it off. The same kestrel flew through the open kitchen window while at hack and proceeded to tuck into the Sunday joint. This did it no harm at all. Another time it was hunting over an adjacent tip when I saw it stoop down and carry something off to its favourite eating post. Its 'quarry' proved to be a mouldy green rind cut from a steak and larded with stale French mustard. It ate this quite happily and repeated the exercise many times over its life.

The lesson to learn from these tales is that the average bird of prey can digest pretty near anything and survive. I sometimes think that if you pushed your finger down their throats, there would only be your boots left as evidence!

Food Storage

You will need freezer space, probably in a second-hand chest freezer in the garage. Do not ever refreeze any food that has already been thawed. If food has been thawed it can be kept cool for a day or two in the fridge if your family let you. After that just throw it away.

Commercially Available Foods

Day-Old Cockerels

These are the males of the egg-laying strains of chicken, and are the mainstay of the modern falconer. As adults they are too small and skinny to be worth rearing for meat, so are an unwanted waste product of our egg industry. Commercially reared chickens are sex-linked to colour and can be sexed as they hatch. The brown chicks are hens, while the cocks are pale yellow and are speedily gassed with carbon dioxide. They are available in huge numbers and at a very reasonable price.

As far as food value is concerned they are the bird of prey equivalent of hay for horses, that is, a low-protein bulk food that will maintain a bird in good health, while not necessarily providing sufficient nourishment to enable it to perform at a higher level. The more humble hawks, such as the buteos (and owls) can do perfectly well on them. Birds that are expected to give higher performance need 'higher octane' fuel.

With all birds of prey I would recommend feeding day-old cockerels during the training period. This is for two reasons. Firstly, they can be counted and it is therefore easy to measure your bird's daily intake. This is important, as by recording this you will establish a regime for your hawk. Secondly, your new hawk is unlikely to become too wayward on such a humble diet. Once the training is better established, and you are working your falcon or accipiter harder, it would be advantageous to move it on to a richer food.

Falconers tend to look down on day-old cockerels. I do not know why. The nutritional breakdown shows that they offer much the same value as chicken, quail and pheasant. There are two potential problems with feeding a constant diet of chicks. The bones are very soft and your bird's beak may, therefore, need coping (trimming) at regular intervals, and secondly, they contain a yolk sac. This is little more than a packed lunch to tide the baby chick over its first day or so, and is full of good nourishment. It also provides an easily digested fluid food, the value of which should not be dismissed when looking after sick birds. Some falconers remove the yolk sac as they fear it can go off. I would suggest that, if they suspect this might be the case, they should not feed any of that particular chick to their hawk. There is also some suspicion that constantly giving day-old cockerels complete with yolk sac can lead to an over-supply of cholesterol. I had one falcon that developed cheesy growths across its body, which were attributed to an excess of cholesterol in its system. However, none of my other hawks have ever shown this problem. and some of them have been with me for twenty years or so.

Grown-Ons and Turkey Poults
Of no significantly different food value than day-olds, these are chicks that have been reared for an extra couple of weeks and are bigger. They do not have yolk sacs and have harder bones. They are more expensive and in shorter supply.

Mice and Rats
Commercially available mice and rats are either surplus to laboratory needs or may have been specifically bred for raptor and reptile food. The meat is much redder (therefore offering better food value) than the equivalent weight of poultry. I feed mice whole but remove the guts from rats. Their stomach contents smell particularly vile, probably because of the food they are given. Some birds do not relish rat, and will flick it away; it certainly looks quite greasy. The tough skin and bones give good exercise to a hawk.

These rodents are comparatively expensive to buy, but I would recommend having a few in stock as a pick-me-up for your hawk.

Quail
Some quail are reared specifically for raptors, others are ex-layers and are often cheaper. They offer good food value and hard bones, and hawks of all types relish them. As with rats and mice it is good to have a few in the freezer.

Food From the Wild
The enterprising falconer should have a continuous supply of hawk food provided by the bird itself. Although I will deal with the individual prey species elsewhere, it is necessary to include their various advantages and disadvantages from a food perspective.

Rabbit
I give the rabbit pride of place because it is, by a very considerable margin, the most frequently hawked animal in Britain. The muscle meat is said to be of little nutritional value. I am not a biochemist or a nutritionist, but my own hunting hawks are fed almost exclusively on

rabbit throughout the hunting season and for the bulk of their rations while they are moulting. They have never suggested to me that they lack strength or stamina, nor have I had any reason to be critical of their feather quality.

While I use mostly muscle meat when out hunting, the hawks have their daily ration completed with a split rabbit head or a piece of the liver or kidneys. This element of 'blood' seems to benefit their condition. You always find the meat is bloodiest where the rabbit has been 'necked', and I try to ensure all the birds get their share of this titbit.

I am conscious of the need to provide as good a diet as possible. To this end I always give a **gorge day** to my hawks at least every ten days and usually more frequently. This is when the hawk is allowed to eat its fill, but is then starved on the following day. The birds that are to be rested get the organs, head and bloody bits and these are fed still warm if at all possible.

As a general rule I find that a female Harris hawk in hard work (a daily minimum of three hours hunting) will need the equivalent of the meat off a rabbit's hind leg, while a male will be fine on the meat equivalent of a front leg. I do not feed the bone, as this is quite nourishing and will put weight on the hawk. Sometimes it is difficult to gauge how much is needed to complete a day's ration when you have been giving small rewards all day to the hawk. Measure out the daily ration at the start of the day, so that what little is left completes the amount. Often it seems a scant reward, but this is only because the bird has been eating all day. In really cold weather your hawk will relish the hot fat from around the kidneys of a freshly gutted rabbit.

Feeding fur-covered carcasses, or even portions, does get the new hawk familiar with its intended quarry. Wherever possible use prey species for food.

Pheasant and Partridge

This is excellent food for your raptor but you may have other ideas. Eat the body yourself but give your bird the head and neck on one day, and on the next the gizzard, liver, heart and lungs. You must remove the shotgun pellets from shot birds. There is less danger of lead poisoning now that steel is the preferred metal used in shotgun cartridges, but it can still happen. I have had a hawk die in spasm from this, after gorging on a decaying carcass that had been left above ground by a thoughtless sportsman.

As with rabbit there is a training value in feeding potential quarry.

Road Carcasses

These are plentiful in game-rich areas. Pheasants, especially, have no road sense and a positive death wish. There is little likelihood of them having ingested pesticides or poison (*see* cat kills, below), but it may be wisest to remove head, guts and organs to be on the safe side. If the carcass is underweight and thin you must assume the pheasant was suffering from an infection or disease which may, just, be transferable to your hawk. Anything that comes into this category usually ends up in my ferret run, in the belief that such a disease is unlikely to transmit across to a mammal. So far my faith in this reasoning has been justified.

Hare and Venison

I have grouped these together as the meat has much the same value. It is always exceedingly dark and strongly flavoured, and of tremendous benefit to ailing, breeding or moulting birds (that is, any bird that is suffering a challenge to its normal state of health). As a food for flying birds, however, it is not recommended. Such dark meat is like rocket fuel and should certainly not be used if you intend to fly your hawk or falcon again tomorrow.

Pigeon

Pigeon is one of the best meats for pepping a bird up. I feed a lot of pigeon in the breeding aviaries and to my moulting birds. Again it is very stimulating and is not suitable for any buteo that is expected to fly the next day. I do sometimes give it to my falcons and accipiters as part of their daily ration if I feel their work has gone 'a bit flat'. They have a faster metabolism and need higher octane fuel, particularly in cold weather.

As with pheasant and partridge, remember to remove all pellets from the carcass and do not use any thin carcasses or ones with greasy ceres/wattles (the fleshy base of the beak). Pigeons can also be vectors of 'frounce', a respiratory infection that is fatal to birds of prey as well. Fortunately the virus is sensitive to cold and can be readily destroyed by freezing the carcass overnight. Once thawed it will be perfectly safe to give to your hawk, despite scare-mongering rumours that it needs to be kept frozen for weeks or even months.

Wildfowl and Waterbirds

These offer good feeding but the same precautions exist regarding shot or thin carcasses. Moorhens are often caught by hawks and are very palatable. The dark flesh tastes sweet and hawks relish it. A moorhen's carcass will feed a male Harris hawk for four days, a female for three. If you can you should skin moorhens. The skin is quite oily and supposedly lowers the condition of your hawk; mine usually leave this anyway.

Cat Kills

The resident cats in your neighbourhood will kill a wide range of the smaller animals and birds on the British list. Their well-intentioned owners may send the children round with carefully packaged offerings to give to your bird. Thank them kindly and put them in the bin – you may find that instead of giving your hawk a tasty meal you have actually given it the poison that caused the creature to be vulnerable in the first place.

Many people put down poison if there are rats or mice about. Equally, keen gardeners have a continuing war with slugs and snails, and use slug bait. Thrushes and blackbirds can just as easily ingest slug pellets at second hand. These are the ones most easily caught by the cats or hit by cars.

Water

Birds of prey get most of their fluid requirements from their victims, which are about 80 per cent water. It is not usual to see them drink (called bowsing or boozing). When they do they will take only three or four sips, so it is not worth supplying a specific source of drinking water. As long as a hawk has access to a clean bath it will help itself when the need arises.

Some birds drink more regularly than others, while some never seem to need water at all. Hot weather encourages drinking and in warmer climates drinking may be seen more frequently. I have a falcon that never bathes (except for dust baths) and ignores its bath when it is thirsty. Instead it will make a beeline for some filthy, oily puddle, usually in the middle of a bus route, and sit there happily trying to decide if it actually wants a drink or not!

Tirings

This term comes from the French verb tirer (to pull). Tirings are any sort of tough, stringy bit of a carcass that the hawk is given on the starvation day following a gorge. It will pull at the tiring, trimming its beak and exercising its back and neck muscles at the same time. The idea is simply to occupy it.

Rangle

You may come across this term, which describes the small, smooth pebbles that were given to hawks in the old days. This was done in an attempt to break up internal fat, when the hawk was being slimmed down after spending the summer moulting. The old falconers believed that the pebbles would be regurgitated, covered in slime or fat, and this would speed up the whole process.

In the spirit of experiment I tried this on one occasion. I force-fed six tiny, smooth pebbles to three of my falcons. The next morning there were six pebbles (totally devoid of fat) beneath two of the blocks. Under the third there were only three pebbles. As my birds were weathered on a gravel base I thought nothing more about it, assuming the missing three would be brought up over the course of that day. Some weeks later I found the three pebbles under the bird's perch, again innocent of any suggestion of fat.

This taught me two lessons. Firstly that rangle does not remove fat from a hawk's system (internal fat is principally deposited around the inside of the body cavity, not the inside of the digestive system). Secondly, although a hawk is capable of regurgitating quite heavy objects, these may remain within its system for a considerable time. I mention this because it has great relevance when feeding carcasses containing shot.

Supplements
There are various vitamin and mineral supplements on the market that are specifically formulated for raptors. Unfortunately most vitamins deteriorate pretty quickly, so they may be of limited value after quite a short while. Therefore it is best to buy in very small quantities, or group together to share out a larger volume.

If you feed your hawk on fresh, warm kills it will get all the additives it requires. Sadly, many birds of prey are not hunted regularly and have a need for supplements. Even so, it is important not to overdose the bird; give small quantities only. When I feed supplements I just dust a chick, or whatever their meal is to consist of, in the supplement powder, and enough sticks to the outside to satisfy their needs. I do this no more than once per week, and usually less frequently.

HYGIENE

Birds of prey have a great tolerance for filth. In the wild their nests may be full of droppings, addled eggs, the desiccated corpses of dead young and the remains of their many victims.

Add a generous mixture of feathers and pellets and then reuse the same nest site for years and years. It sounds a recipe for disaster.

Admittedly the more open nests (or eyries) are cleaned by the action of frost, rain, sun, snow and wind. All the same they are far removed from the ideal of cleanliness that an old-fashioned hospital matron might aspire to. Yet wild birds of prey always look immaculate.

The same is true in captivity. Raptors require peace and quiet if they are to breed successfully. This means that their breeding aviaries are seldom entered by the breeder, and only cleaned at the start and finish of each breeding season. I remember ringing a nest full of young barn owls. They were their parent's second brood of the year, so the nest box was fairly filthy. After a couple of days I went to check that the rings were still in place. It was as well that I took this precaution, as one had slipped off the foot of the smallest owlet. To find the missing ring I had to sift through the floor of the nest with my fingers. There were things living there that science had probably not got a name for.

So hygiene is not a major requirement of the healthy bird of prey. However, you will probably have neighbours who want to enjoy their gardens without the attentions of clouds of bluebottles and a smell akin to a maggot factory. They may also be unhappy if your aviaries attract rats, a not uncommon occurrence when there are pieces of food and pellets liberally strewn across the floor.

All this changes if your bird is in low condition and is susceptible to infection. Nature may not care if weak individuals succumb to disease, but you may if it is your bird, and if it has been weakened by your lack of judgement or care. Therefore, hygiene is necessary as a precautionary measure.

Food Containers
Clean out and disinfect your freezer periodically (every three or four months). Wash any food containers and preparation areas daily and use containers that can be closed while food is

thawing. This will make it difficult for flies to get in and lay their eggs.

Mews

If you house your hawk in a mews building you will need to clean this regularly. My own birds are perched over newspaper, which is picked up and removed on a daily basis. Beneath this is a layer of plastic sheeting, which is given a quick daily wipe over and is changed once a week (some faeces always manage to miss the paper). The perch surface is scrubbed each day, when the hawks are put out to weather, with a weak solution of household bleach.

Since my mews is made of wooden sections there is a risk that red mites may take up residence in the many cracks in the walls, and they can be an insidious menace. Your bird's performance slowly gets poorer, but the deterioration is so gradual that it takes time to realize that any problem exists. It may lose weight and become lethargic. Although you may not be able to see anything amiss, it is worth checking if it has a mite infestation. This is simply a matter of visiting the mews at night and inspecting your bird by torchlight (and, in my case, with the help of reading glasses). You may see lots of tiny red dots moving about on its cere and around its eyes. These are the mites and they are blood-sucking parasites. Closer inspection of your hawk's mouth may reveal that it no longer displays a healthy pink colour but has become anaemic.

The remedy is fairly simple. There are anti-mite preparations on the market, as racing pigeons can have the same problem. Some of these can be administered directly on to the hawk, while others are used to treat all the wooden surfaces in which the mites shelter during daylight hours. An ingenious way of checking for mites is simply to wrap double-sided sticky tape around the base of the perch, which can then be checked for visitors.

Since prevention is better than cure, it is sensible to wash the mews walls, and perches, with an anti-mite solution about every six months.

Aviary

The hawk that is being free-lofted in an aviary can deposit its droppings widely. However, these will mostly be under its favourite perches, or liberally plastered down the wall behind them. Removing them from the ground may be a problem if you have a gravel base to the aviary. Instead you should keep a rake in the aviary, to break up any accumulation of faeces, and at the same time pick up any pellets, feathers and bones that may be left from the hawk's meals. Then roughly disinfect the floor area by spraying with a weak bleach solution or a raptor-specific disinfectant. This will keep the aviary smelling sweet and will also deter weeds from sprouting everywhere.

Because aviaries are outside they are often used as perching places by other garden birds. This increases the risk of mite infestation, which will need the same rigorous treatment as you applied in the mews. If, as recommended, the perches are of natural branches, these should be changed every six months and scrubbed most days. The bark is a natural hiding place for mites, so scrub them before installing them.

Weathering Ground

Your hawk is pretty immobile in the weathering ground and faeces build up if you do not rake the gravel regularly. As with the aviary floor you will also need to spray the gravel. This, and cleaning the perches and baths, should be a daily chore. Certainly you should not leave it more than a week.

Remember to treat any timber areas of the weathering ground against mites.

Gloves and Hawking Bags

Both these items of equipment quickly accumulate dirt. A layer of blood, egg yolk (if you feed chicks) and other unidentified filth may turn your soft, supple gauntlet into a heavy, rigid lump that falls to the ground with a noticeable thump. Use your knife on a daily basis to scrape the worst of this off. You can also scrub the affected surfaces with an old nail brush and warm soapy water. Unfortunately doing this may remove the natural oils from the leather so that it goes hard. A regular (weekly) light wiping with leather dressing will restore the leather, and is quickly soaked up so that the glove does not become slippery and therefore a security risk in its own right.

Sometimes I wash my gloves. To prevent them from becoming hard when they dry, I rinse them out in a bowl of warm water on which is floating a fairly generous film of leather dressing oil. I prefer to use Hydrophane Leather Dressing (available from saddlery shops) as this is very light and does not make the glove too greasy. A greasy glove can be quite clammy to wear and also soon develops a smell of its own.

Bags (and waistcoats) are used for storing meat to reward the hawk with, and for carrying your quarry. Dead animals and birds have a habit of leaving blood and urine in the bottom of your bag. Falconers also tend to leave small pieces of meat there and forget them. It is much more pleasant to clean the bag out at the end of each day, than to find before your next outing that it contains a healthy population of maggots. The outside of bags can also become very muddy or marked with blood, lichen, rabbit droppings and the like.

Fortunately bags are made of canvas or some similar washable material. Soak them overnight in soapy water and then scrub them thoroughly. Hang them up inside out to dry. The domestic washing machine will do an excellent job but it may be better not to let the rest of the family discover that you are doing this!

MAINTENANCE

The maintenance of all equipment and facilities is an ongoing chore, and since exercising the hawk always takes priority, it does tend to get pushed a little further back in the order of things. I have already recommended the relevant materials for treating wooden surfaces and brick or concrete buildings in the section on the design and fabrication of mews, weathering ground and aviary. Bear in mind, however, that while well-maintained facilities should last for longer they will not last forever. Although it is a long way ahead in your falconry career, do not join the band of us who have made stupid mistakes and suffered losses because we believed that the 'broken hinge will be OK', or 'the netting will last a bit longer'. Do keep on top of maintenance.

ROUTINE TASKS

Casting a Bird of Prey

From the day when you return home and equip your new bird, and for all those occasions when it will require restraint while you carry out minor tasks, it will be necessary to cast your bird, that is, to hold it bodily. If the bird is not jessed up you may first have to catch it or put a towel or coat over it. Once it is immobilized it needs to be held securely, not just to prevent it escaping but also to avoid anybody getting scratched, bitten or footed.

With a bird that is jessed up and sitting on the fist you may be able to gather it in against your body before actually getting a firm grip of it. Many falconers advise holding the hawk in a towel to prevent loss of the weatherproofing in the bird's feathers. They also recommend letting it grip a cushion or something equally soft, so that it does not grip and injure its own feet.

Personally I would rather have a secure hold on the bird. Casting is such an occasional thing that I do not believe the feather damage is measurable. On the other hand, the damage to you or your assistant may be quite appreciable if a foot gets free. To hold a bird securely I like to have its legs between the first

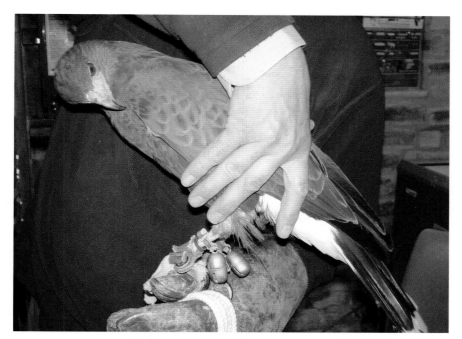

Preparing to cast a trained hawk from the glove. This is less stressful than someone else approaching it to grab it.

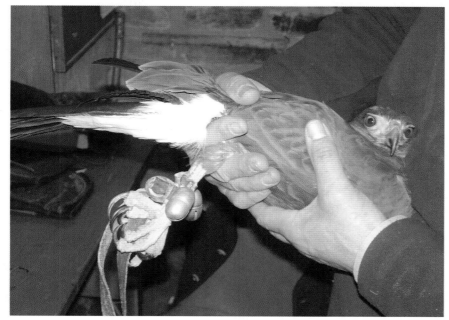

Anyone holding a cast hawk must restrain the wings and have total control over the feet.

two fingers of my hand, with the base of the tail and the wings circled by my thumb and forefinger . The bird's body will then be lying in the palm of your hand. To stop it slipping forward you simply cradle its head against your body, using your other hand to keep the bird supported and to immobilize the wings. Held like this it is easy for the assistant to extend each leg separately to fit anklets and bells, treat bites and abrasions, trim talons and so on. The other leg remains under control.

Feather Care

Feather Mites and Lice

The presence of these may be spotted where you can see that the webbing on feathers has been eaten away. Treatment with any proprietorial lice and mite spray, as used by pigeon racers, cage bird breeders and so on, is quite suitable.

Bent Feathers

From time to time your hawk, falcon or owl may bend feathers. Almost invariably these will be flight or tail feathers and therefore important. There are feather straighteners you can buy from equipment suppliers for use in the field, or, once home, you can simply dip the damaged feathers in hand-hot water for a few seconds. The feather will immediately return to its proper shape.

Broken Feathers

More dramatic than the bent feather is the one that is broken completely. It may be hanging by a thread or may have snapped off altogether. Again it is the major feathers that are important. The process of repairing them is called imping.

Feathers that are growing are full of blood and will bleed profusely. If one of these breaks you should wait until the remaining stump of feather is fully mature. At this stage it will consist of hard, dead tissue, similar to our fingernails or hair. The spine of the feather is a hollow tube. This allows you to fasten the two broken halves together by inserting a central pin of some sort. Traditionally steel or iron needles (imping needles) were used. Because these were quite rigid the feather had a new stress point at each end of the needle, and was therefore prone to break again. For tail feathers I use guitar strings, the sort that are coiled, as this gives a secure hold and will

also flex with the natural spring of the feather. Wing feathers are more difficult as they are much broader on the trailing edge than the leading one. In flight this means that the feather exerts unequal pressure on either side of the central spine. The imped feather will then tend to rotate around the guitar wire, making the repair totally useless. For these feathers I use pieces of carbon fibre fishing rods, which I can shape to give an elliptical cross-section. This still flexes but prevents the feather from rotating.

The procedure is simple. Take the broken piece of feather and insert a pin of guitar wire or carbon fibre that just fits tightly in the spine without splitting it. Cover the exposed end with contact adhesive. Then, with someone holding the bird, slide the glued end in to the broken stump of feather that is still in the bird. The whole operation takes only a minute or two, and the only thing that distresses the bird – being held – is over in seconds.

Sometimes your hawk may have broken the feather while hunting and you cannot find it. Ideally you will have saved last year's moulted feathers and can simply select the identical one as a replacement. With a young bird you may not have any such spares, and will have to resort to a similar feather from another bird. My falcons can often be seen sporting a feather from a different species, but my favourite imping story concerns one of my kestrels.

This particular bird was badly imprinted and would mantle over any food. It would press its tail feathers across my glove and, over a period of time, managed to break every single one. I continued to fly it but the lack of tail made it desperately unbalanced. Its coping strategy was to go flat out. It became a jet-propelled kestrel. Landing involved flying upwards towards its intended perch until, at just the right moment, it lost all its impetus and was able to stop.

Having exhausted my stock of spare feathers I looked around for a suitable replacement. By chance I found a wood

Imping broken feathers is surprisingly quick and easy.

pigeon that was carrying a donor card. These feathers were bigger and heavier than I needed, but were much more robust. I was able to trim them down so that they matched the originals quite closely, and I have to say that it was the best imping job I have ever done. Each feather laid over its neighbour perfectly, and the join was so high up that it was hidden under the tail coverts. The kestrel could flex and fan them perfectly.

The first time it went out with its new tail it flew at its usual speed. After a while it decided to land, and aimed for a favourite branch. With a look of total consternation on its face it stopped about a metre short and missed the branch altogether. On its next approach it managed a successful, but very cautious, landing.

I was at a show, with the kestrel on its little block, when an ardent birdwatcher came by. For several minutes he studied the tiny falcon. Eventually he could no longer contain his curiosity.

'What kind of bird is that? I know my birds pretty well, and it looks like some kind of kestrel, but I can't place it.'

'It's a British bird,' I assured him.

'No it can't be. There's no British bird that looks like that.'

'It really is, it's a wood kestrel.' When I explained the 'trick' he went away a very relieved birdspotter indeed.

HEALTH AND ILL HEALTH

Given that you bought your hawk from a good breeder, and that you have a clean home for it and exercise it adequately in return for a sufficient quantity of good quality food, you can reasonably expect your hawk to remain healthy. And most of the time this will be the case. Sometimes, however, despite your best efforts, things may go wrong. At this time it is important to be aware that you are your bird's first line of defence. Nobody knows it better than you do, or observes it more closely. Nobody else will be as sensitive to small, subtle changes in its behaviour or bearing that might suggest that all is not well. For this reason you should learn to recognize the symptoms of good health in your bird.

You should carry out a daily health check that starts each morning the moment you walk down the garden to the aviary or mews. Early recognition of ill health is vital. The bird of prey, despite being captive-bred, is fundamentally wild. The last thing a wild creature does, to avoid attracting predators, is display any sign of weakness. For this reason your bird will mask its illness, sometimes so effectively that the first symptom can be death itself. Be aware.

Posture

Is it perched where it normally does? Is it greeting you as you have come to expect? (One of my current team chirps as I enter, and bobs up and down to me, while its neighbour drops a threatening shoulder and curses me. I would be concerned if either behaved untypically.) When you weigh it or carry it to its perch, does it step lightly on to the glove and sit in its usual stance? Does it automatically perch on the highest point of the bow perch? You may not consciously check these points but you should subconsciously spot anything different.

The hawk that sits on the ground instead of its perch, and that is not standing erect, is in a bad way. Lethargic movement, low head carriage, general apathy and fluffed-out feathers add to a sad picture. If your bird is exhibiting any of these symptoms you should get it to a specialist bird of prey vet as soon as possible.

Mutes

Everybody who keeps livestock develops an obsession with their animal's motions. A daily inspection of these is an important aspect of checking on their wellbeing. Because you have made a practice of cleaning soiled areas, you can be sure that only the droppings from the last twenty-four hours are visible. This means that any change is easily observed.

All diurnal raptors should produce a lot of faeces. These normally comprise a majority of chalky white fluid (the avian equivalent of urine), within which is a more solid, dark brown or black deposit. The buteos and accipiters can propel these huge distances when being fed a full ration of food. Their propulsive powers wane when they are on a diet, so the scope of the distribution is governed by the amount of food they have received and not by their health.

Owls will produce similar-coloured droppings for the most part but have the ability to occasionally produce a large, sloppy, foul-smelling pool of a fairly unattractive brown. This is usually evident first thing in the morning but they do not keep to a predictable timetable on this. Both types of droppings are normal for owls.

When your bird is not in good health you may notice that the faeces are green (of varying shades) and sometimes frothy. They may also be blood-stained. These are all indicative of diarrhoea or possibly enteritis. If you are particularly keen-eyed you may also find that the mutes are excessively liquid with a waxy surface. In all cases contact your specialist vet immediately, taking a sample with you. This should comprise the dark centre of the faeces from the last twenty-four hours.

Pellets

Pellets are formed within the crop from the fur or feather of the hawk's victims or food ration. They cleanse the crop like a scouring pad. Owls form them rather differently as they have no crop. Instead the pellet is formed, rather like a cat's fur ball, within the owl's stomach, and it is coughed up as a package within which are held the indigestible bones and teeth of its prey.

However, in all birds of prey the pellets should be of a firm consistency (that is, capable of being picked up without losing shape). Although slimy when first produced they should quickly dry out and become very

Pellets should be well-formed and dry out quickly.

light. The colour of a healthy pellet should be that of the fur or feather on the hawk's previous meal. Pellets that are sloppy may simply reflect that the food had a high water content. Remedy this by feeding a drier meal next time and observing the subsequent pellet. If it is still sloppy and unformed, consult your vet.

Of greater concern is the bird of prey (owls excepted) that regurgitates a pellet containing some undigested matter. This may be caused by the hawk having been given a second feed during the preceding day (for example if you are trying to encourage a speedy moult). Take this as a warning sign and stop the practice. A bird that has not had sufficient time to clear its crop out before being given more food is in danger of developing an impacted crop, which can be fatal.

Especially when you are reducing your hawk's weight, either at the start of its training or when retraining it for a new season, you may find that its pellet is very small. This reflects the reduced quantity of food it has been having, and the pellet may well be tinged with green. Where this has occurred you can be sure that the bird's system is pretty nearly empty. What has caused this colour is the bile, which is all that is left in its stomach. If I see a green-tinged pellet in a young hawk I am training, I would expect a quick response in training. Unless this happens it is wise to give the bird a gorge for a day or so before recommencing the training.

Appetite

Any bird of prey that is at a normal flying weight will eat with considerable gusto, tearing at its food and gulping down unexpectedly large lumps. It should not stop eating while there is food left, or until it is completely full (gorged). If you hawk displays inappetence, that is, refusing food when it should be hungry, or flicks its food away, you must assume it is gravely ill. You will need professional help. You bird may well need antibiotics or crop-tubing (*see* below).

External Examination

Eyes

The most significant feature of the bird of prey's head is its eyes. These should be bright, round and continually reacting to visual stimuli. The pupil will contract and expand as it focuses on different things around it. This is instinctive and necessary self-protection. A bird that does not do this may very well be 'tired of life'. A dull eye, lack of eye movement and an elliptical eye shape are all cause for concern.

You may observe a changed eye shape during the early stages of training, when the bird is being most severely disciplined with hunger. This is also when a new hawk is at its most frightened, and its eyes are usually wide open with fright. Being unused to your fist, it will look alert despite feeling pretty low. Observed on its perch from a distance, it will often appear worse. This is normal, and if this symptom is present you really have got the bird as thin as you need. Most young birds will get to this point before they condescend to eat from the fist.

Sometimes only one eye will be narrowed. If this is accompanied by a visible swelling of the face below the eye, and a perceptible movement of the skin over that area as the bird breathes, it may be indicative of sinusitis.

The trained bird will sometimes injure an eye. This could be as dramatic as puncturing an eye on a thorn, or being bitten by rat, stoat or squirrel. A severe blow may cause a lens to dislocate. Often it is no more than a scratch to the surface of the eye, but if one eye is not reacting to light or movement, or if you see any scarring to the surface, you must get veterinary advice. To put this risk in perspective, I have never had such an injury to any of my hunting birds.

Mouth

Watch carefully when your hawk is eating, or simply prise open its beak if you are confident you can cast (hold) it properly and securely. The inside of the mouth should be pink. If it is very pale this indicates anaemia, possibly resulting from parasite overload (mites or worms) or internal bleeding. I do not send faeces samples for worm checks. Instead I administer worm medicine routinely, at the start and end of each hunting season.

The mouth should also be free of cheesy growths or ulceration.

Occasionally a bird of prey may repeatedly gape (a yawning action). This may be caused

Examining the mouth usually requires an assistant to hold the hawk.

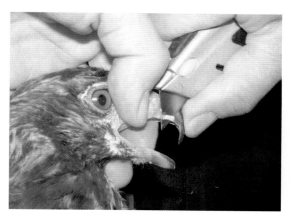

Coping a hawk's beak with a craft knife to take off excess growth; it has probably been neglected to reach this stage.

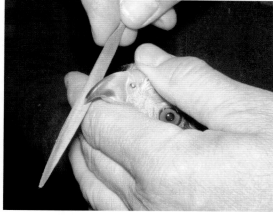

Filing a hawk's beak to shape after coping or as a routine task to prevent excess growth.

by an obstruction in its throat, such as a sharp piece of bone. You may be lucky enough to be able to remove this yourself, otherwise you would need to get veterinary help. Another cause for this behaviour may be the presence of gape worms in your bird's throat. These parasites affect poultry, and the earthworm is their intermediate host. If your bird eats worms and there are chickens around, it may have contracted this infestation. Treatment is with standard poultry medication at the strength advised by your vet.

Beak

Just like our fingernails, the beak of a bird of prey grows slowly throughout its life. The action of tearing its prey and breaking up small bones should keep it trimmed. In captivity we often give soft food in the form of day-old chicks or lumps of meat. This means the beaks of our birds tend to get overgrown, not just in length but in thickness. A badly overgrown beak may need to be trimmed down (coped), with a craft knife or a scalpel, to get it back to something approaching its proper proportions. Then, and at other times, it can be filed to shape with a half-round key file, or even a nail file. Always check that you have coped the beak evenly on both sides.

Falcon's beak in need of coping. Often a split will run up from the notch in the beak towards the nostril.

Failure to do this could result in a twisted or lopsided beak.

Some hawks will have beaks that split or flake away. This argues a lack of vitamins, minerals or trace elements in its diet, so introduce a daily supplement for about a week, and continue this on a regular weekly basis. Where a beak has split badly you will have to trim it as far back as the start of the split. As the beak regrows keep checking that it is growing in its proper shape, filing it to maintain this. The falcons suffer most from splits that run up from the notch in the beak towards the nostril. Hawks and buteos can get very long tips on their beaks and flaky sides.

It is important to shape the side of an overgrown beak. If you simply snip of the end you will have a much broader beak left, which will overgrow even more quickly. Usually it is only the top beak that needs trimming, but if this grows out too straight it will not rub against the lower jaw (mandible) and this too may need attention. In my experience this never needs more than the lightest of filing jobs.

Cere
This is the fleshy base to the beak, and should be of a similar colour to the feet of the bird. This will usually be a shade of yellow, although some species of falcons have blue or even red feet and owls may have grey or black feet. In all cases the cere should not be greasy, nor should there be a discharge from the nostrils (nares). Sometimes you may observe a bruising around the cere (a more orange tinge to the flesh). This indicates the possible presence of blood-sucking mites (see Mews, under Hygiene, above).

Feathers
Healthy feathers lie close to the bird's body and, while not glossy, should have a discernible bloom, rather like that on a ripe plum. They should also be fairly weather resistant, a factor which will vary from species to species. As a normal rule you would expect species from wet or temperate climates to be better in this respect than species from desert regions. Nevertheless each bird will have better 'rain-proofing when it is in robust good health. Over time your experience with caring for your own bird will enable you to notice if there is any difference in its feather quality. This may depend on the quality of moult that your bird has experienced: the more vigorous the feather loss and growth, the better feather quality you might expect for the subsequent year.

The signs you definitely do not want to see are feathers hanging loosely or standing up over its head. Invariably this will be accompanied by poor posture. If, in addition to this, your bird has difficulty in keeping itself dry, you should improve the quality of its food for a week or two, including laying it off work for a while. If you find this hard to do, you can console yourself that your bird would probably have performed badly in any case. At least it is still alive, and you have only yourself to blame, by working it too hard and not feeding it adequately.

Broken and bent feathers are a fact of life for working birds of prey. They rarely occur in wild raptors because they do not have to tackle such big quarry or take such risks of injury. In captivity some species, particularly the accipiters, can end the season resembling a broken feather duster. Feather care is covered under Routine Tasks.

Feet and Legs
The captive bird of prey is prone to foot problems. The supply of blood to the foot is not good, so if the foot becomes infected it is difficult to deliver antibiotics to the area. Great strides have been made with this in recent years but the basic difficulty remains. Any trauma to the foot can result in infection and you must be constantly vigilant. The condition is known as bumblefoot. This describes any swollen, heated foot condition and is a symptom only. Your job is to get the problem sorted out before this symptom is even visible.

Falcons are particularly susceptible to developing pressure sores from continually having to perch on the same even surface. This is why you should offer varied surfaces for them. The hawks and buteos, which tend to still-hunt more in the wild, have tougher feet that are naturally more resilient to this. However, these hawks are the most likely to catch animals that may retaliate, and bites and scratches are just as likely to let infection in. It

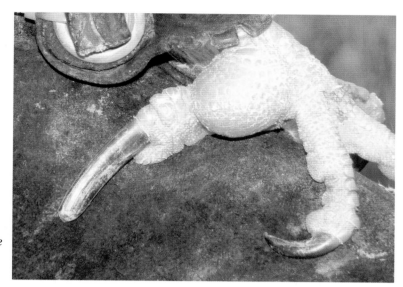

Faulty growth of broken talon. You can see a bumblefoot on the side of the bird's foot caused by the same hunting injury.

is worth your while to carry a disinfectant spray of wound dressing powder (available from chemists), to treat immediately any injury your bird may pick up. There is no point in waiting until you get home as the wound will have sealed itself in about twenty minutes, sealing in any infection at the same time.

A hunting bird of prey may also break a talon or even rip it out. Providing the quick (the fleshy and sensitive core of the talon) is not damaged the talon will eventually grow back. If the quick is also pulled out the talon will never grow back, while any lesser damage may result in a talon growing back in an incorrect shape. Judicious trimming may help in this latter case. One of the causes of birds losing talons is that, having been in an aviary during the moult, their talons have overgrown. Unless these are trimmed before they re-commence hunting, the leverage is too great and can lead to them breaking off. When trimming over-long talons just snip the tips off (by no more than 3mm/^{1}/$_8$in for a Harris) and file back into a point.

An infected injury will make the foot and/or leg become hot and sometimes swollen. The colour may differ discernibly from the other leg. Perhaps the bird carries that foot, or shows a reluctance to put weight on it. You must get it attended to at once. Your vet should take a swab from the infected site, so that a culture can be prepared to identify the infection and determine the antibiotics to which it may be sensitive. Normally the vet will prescribe a broad spectrum antibiotic while waiting for the results of the swab.

I have had birds that have responded well to initial treatment but then relapsed. On a few occasions this has been where the most evident source of infection has cleared up, only for a second, less evident one, to become apparent. My experience with two male peregrines will illustrate the difficulty that foot problems can create. The first was one of my display birds that had suffered from a pressure sore for some months. It had been treated repeatedly without success. The second was an injured wild bird that was found tangled in a tennis net. This poor creature had a hugely swollen and dislocated leg that was extremely hot.

My own bird continued to exhaust every known treatment that my vet could prescribe. The difficulty was that the only antibiotic specific to that infection was so thick that it could not be delivered to the site. By contrast the wild bird responded to treatment and its infection cleared up in a matter of days. Sadly the damage to its leg was so great that the joint had been eroded away, and euthanasia was the only option. In the end I had the sad experience of going to the vets with two birds and coming back with none.

Birds of prey can also break and dislocate toes, legs, hocks and so on. Sometimes these will set well but the success depends on splinting the foot carefully. The bones are normally much too delicate to permit pinning. Raptors make excellent patients and will happily wear bandages and plasters for weeks without any attempt to pull them off.

YOU AND YOUR VET

Finding the Right Vet
When I first starting keeping birds of prey there were only a handful of veterinary surgeons with any knowledge of birds of prey. Avian knowledge at that time revolved around the poultry industry. A vet would be brought a dead chicken, with the request that he find out how to save the rest of the flock. This is no use to the falconer who wants his one bird saved.

Thanks to the pioneering work of such good people as John Cooper, Mike Williams, Neil Forbes and Nigel Harcourt-Brown we now have a solid base of knowledge, excellent surgical techniques, better drugs and advanced anaesthetics. There are now several specialist veterinary surgeons in Britain. Last year no fewer than thirty-two advertised in the IBR Directory and they can be found in most parts of the country.

It is foolhardy to use a veterinary practice that does not specialize, but you may be forced to. If this is the case you should make sure from the outset that your vet understands the value of your bird, and is prepared to consult with a specialist. Some vets seem reluctant to admit that there can be any area of animal medicine in which they are not an expert. One vet prescribed a powder 'to be put in the bird's drinking water'. When I explained that the birds rarely drank he burst out, 'How the hell was I supposed to know that?'

My own vet, who has a healthy practice in birds of prey, was happy when, on first visiting his surgery, I took with me the only current veterinary book on birds of prey. That bill was paid with a second copy of it for him. The next bill was paid for by a trip to a veterinary conference on the care of raptors. A quarter of a century later, and both a lot greyer around the head, the 'young vit'nary' told me he now treated about two birds of prey a day.

Administering Tablets and Pills
This is really easy. Just hide the pill inside a juicy piece of meat and it will be swallowed before the bird has any chance to taste the contents. I did once have a falcon that was on antibiotics. The first course was unsuccessful so my vet prescribed a different one. Although the pills looked identical the bird knew immediately that they were different and would not take them. We had to cast the bird and force them into its crop instead. I could smell no difference between the two bottles but the falcon, despite its supposedly poor or even non-existent sense of smell, could tell them apart very easily.

Crop-Tubing
This is the process by which fluids or liquidized food can be placed in the bird's system when it will not take them voluntarily. The bird will need to be cast by an assistant while you introduce the tube into the bird's crop. The fluids to be given are held in a normal plastic 5ml or 10ml syringe, which you can get from your veterinary surgeon. Fix a soft length of plastic tubing to the nozzle (I find that the soft tubing used by aquarium keepers for their pumps, or similar gauge tubing from homebrew stores, is ideal). It is important that soft tubing is used so that it will not damage the bird's mouth or throat as it is introduced. This tube should be about 10cm (4in) in length unless you have a very

big hawk. You can gently heat the far end to soften any sharp edges where you have cut it.

While the bird is being held firmly, open its beak wide so that you can see clearly. There will be two orifices. The smaller of the two is under the base of the tongue and is the opening of the windpipe. On no circumstances must you put the feeding tube down this.

The second opening is much larger and is at the back of the mouth, being very distinctly the bird's gullet. By gently straightening the hawk's head and neck to form a straight line, you can easily slide the feeding tube down into the crop. As the tube goes in, you will probably see the outside of the crop bulge. Do this with great care, as it is possible to rupture the crop if this is done too roughly. However, the hawk itself can push sharp bones and other large items down, so the whole thing is pretty resilient. Once the tube is down you can depress the plunger on the syringe to steadily deliver the fluid to the bird. Watch carefully to make sure that the fluid does not come back up the throat and spill into the windpipe.

This treatment is normally only used with a bird in an extremely bad way. Classically this might be a hunting hawk, particularly a delicate accipiter, that has been worked too hard, at too low a body weight, in cold conditions. It will have exhausted its blood glucose and collapsed into a kind of hypoglycaemic coma. The introduction of a warm glucose mixture or electrolyte solution will work wonders in these circumstances. A bird that seemed at death's door may well be back on its feet in half an hour and, given a good feed, should be capable of limited work the next day.

Sometimes a bird of prey becomes so debilitated that it is virtually anorexic, flicking any food away and regurgitating anything forced down its throat. This may be an injured wild bird, but I have had the same experience with young birds that have been lost. By the time they have been found they have lost much of the will to live. Solid food, no matter how readily taken, will do no good at all. They

Crop tubing may be necessary for administering fluid therapy; you must know which is the gullet and which the windpipe.

will have no fluids left inside their stomachs or crops with which to digest anything. Any food will remain undigested, blocking the system and slowly going bad. In a short while the already debilitated bird will die, poisoned by the rotting contents of its stomach. The only course of action is to crop-tube with electrolyte fluids at regular intervals (say every two hours). The liquid is easily absorbed into the bloodstream and, after about a day, there will be sufficient in the digestive system to allow the hawk to be given more sustaining food. This should be in the form of liquidized high-protein food, again administered by crop-tubing. I use Hill's Science Diet for Cats and add a little glucose to the mix. Only after a day on this concentrated ration should you start giving ordinary food.

Milking the Crop

Your hawk may have eaten something that you suspect will harm it, or it may simply have gorged on a kill before you were able to find it. In either case you may wish to milk the crop. This is done by casting the bird, and then gently massaging the contents of the crop back up its gullet, in a kind of enforced regurgitation. It will not thank you for this and, if you are out hunting, will probably sulk for quite some time. It is a procedure to use as little as possible.

In the case of possible poisoning it is sensible to flush the crop out with fluids, taking care that none are able to enter the windpipe as they are forced out.

Hospitalization

From time to time it may be necessary to hospitalize your hawk. Perhaps a leg injury means that it cannot be tethered or left loose in an aviary. It will require close restraint and the best way is to keep it in a dark container, such as a pet carrier with a blanket draped over it, or even a large cardboard box. In both cases keep the bird on vet bed or carpet so that it can lie down on a soft surface. Birds of prey are patient invalids and it is much better to do this than to have them stressed by a succession of fresh sights. It will not be for long, as even a broken bone will heal within two weeks.

An old common buzzard of mine managed to break its thigh very close to its pelvis. The break was so high that it could not be pinned. My vet was gloomy about the outcome, and simply advised me to keep it as still as possible and let nature take its course. In the event the buzzard lay down for two weeks, allowing me to feed it by hand. After that it simply stood up, showing no signs of injury at all. The leg had set absolutely straight.

THE MOULT

When I first started in falconry I was unsure of how important it was to give your bird a good moult. I reasoned that the wild birds of prey seemed to moult out perfectly well without having to be rested. Why then should my own hawk need months of tender care? Moreover, having only just got him hunting well, I was reluctant to finish my season. There were suddenly lots of baby bunnies about with very little cover to conceal them.

Accordingly I kept him going until halfway through April. After that he was put in his aviary and fed as much food, of the very best quality, that I could lay my hands on. To my chagrin he shed not a single feather for the best part of two months. By the start of the next season he still had half his tail and most of his wings to go.

Still fired with enthusiasm I brought his weight down and disregarded his somewhat patchy appearance. We had another good season but he was not as weatherproof. Moreover, it was apparent, as we edged toward the spring, that he was a little jaded. This time I stopped hunting much earlier. By the end of February he was in his aviary. Again it took him two months to recharge his batteries and begin moulting but, being in a less debilitated condition to start with, he was able to complete his moult. When I started hunting him for his third season, he had much better feather quality and was more vigorous altogether.

What every new falconer needs to recognize is that the trained hawk is kept chronically hungry for several months. His reserves will be so seriously depleted that it will take a while before he will have sufficient vigour to change all those feathers. Unless you are prepared to invest in this you will jeopardize the following season.

CHAPTER 5

Buying a Bird of Prey

As you are embarking on a potentially long 'marriage', it is worth spending time at the start to eliminate as many pitfalls as possible. Your facilities should be in place and your equipment ready before you actually set about buying your new hawk. Hopefully you will have found a reliable and helpful guru, and with his help have decided on the species and sex of your bird. You should have covered the following points:

- Select a breeder of good reputation, having asked through your local falconry club, or taken the advice of your mentor/friend.
- Order before the breeding season commences, and put down a deposit if this is required (but get a receipt). Specify the age, sex and rearing regime you want for your bird, for example parent- or creche-reared. Buying a bird later in the summer, or more crucially after the hunting season has commenced, means that you will have less time to establish your training and get your bird fit. This is particularly true in the case of falcons that you intend to fly at game. The later you get your falcon on the wing and ready to enter, the fitter its quarry will be. The young falcon will struggle when matched against fit, experienced game, so it is important to get it entered before the young grouse or partridge become strong and wily. Otherwise it will be at a disadvantage and may easily be disheartened. Nothing succeeds like

success, so try to give your young falcon a winning chance from the outset.
- If you intend leaving the bird in your aviary for a few weeks (recommended with young Harris hawks to minimize any potential parent dependency), have the screening already in place, over any open mesh areas, to prevent the hawk seeing you.
- Organize your time so that you have a few days free at the start of the training programme.

Before going to collect your hawk you should be familiar with your equipment, sure that it is all present, along with the appropriate tools, and that you know how to put it on the bird.

COLLECTING YOUR BIRD

Take a sturdy cardboard box with several air holes punched a couple of centimetres above the base. These low holes give the hawk a continual supply of fresh air but do not offer any visual stimuli so it will remain calm during transit to your home. Place some carpet or towelling on the floor to provide a surface the bird can grip. This is the safest, kindest way of transporting a new bird. You do not want it to thrash about and damage its feathers or to distress itself. Being in the dark it will sit pretty still. Take strong tape to secure the box shut. Also take your glove, jesses, a swivel and leash, and bells. The vendor should be willing to hold the bird while you equip it. This means, too,

Hunger trace mark on a feather can be caused by malnutrition or stress during the growth of that feather. It is a weakness that makes the feather liable to break.

that you will have something to get hold of when you need to extract the bird from the box.

If the hawk is sold as parent-reared you should see the bird in the aviary, with its parents, before you buy it. This is the time to look for any lack of symmetry in its wing carriage or posture, denoting injuries or deformities that may be permanent. Only when you are happy with this visual inspection should you ask the breeder to catch it up because, if it damages itself at this stage, the bird is still his property. He should allow you to examine it before you equip it or place it in the box.

First Examination

Although you will have little experience to go on you may as well feel the hawk's breast to make sure that it is fairly plump. This will vary from species to species (some peregrines, for example, have very pronounced, deep keels, so may appear much thinner than they really are), but at least it will give you a starting point with which to make subsequent comparisons. This is the fattest your hawk is likely to be for some months, and it should feel decidedly powerful across its shoulders.

Tail and Wing Feathers
All these should be present and complete. Sometimes, especially with birds that have been in the aviary for some time, there may be some tiny 'chips' from the ends of feathers. This is acceptable but undesirable. Look also for any hairline 'trace' marks across the major feathers. These represent stress periods or checks in the bird's growth. If they are clearly visible the spine of the feathers will be probably pinched at that point (this is easily detected by running your fingers down the quill). An appreciable narrowing means the feather is weakened and will certainly break very easily, so you should avoid such a bird. It has not been reared well.

Feet
Feet may be quite dirty as breeding aviaries are not cleaned during the season. Gently remove any accumulation of dirt and look for cuts or abrasions. There should be no heat or swelling, particularly in the ball of the foot. Count that all the toes and talons are present and complete. This sounds silly, but remember 'no foot, no hawk'. Bowed legs denote rickets

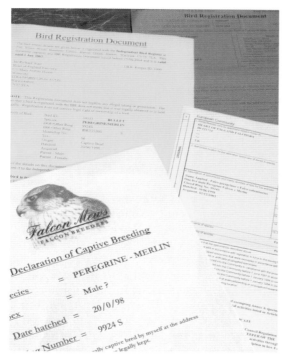

Legally required documentation varies according to species and country of origin.

IBR closed rings are individually numbered and are the best way to identify a lost bird.

– if you spot this, do not buy the bird. A good breeder gives sufficient supplements and good-quality food to avoid this condition.

Head
The eyes will be bright and round because the bird is terrified. Normally the eyes are a good indicator of health but you will need to wait until the bird is relaxed before they can be of any help. Its mouth will probably be gaping open and it will be panting. Look to see if the inside is pink and free from any growths. Also the fleshy base of the beak (the cere) should not be greasy.

Ring Number
If it has no closed ring on you should not buy the bird – nor if the ring number does not tally with subsequent paperwork!

Documentation
All captive bred birds of prey should be close ringed, and the ring should have a permanent, unique serial number on it. In addition you should receive and retain:

- A breeder's letter certifying the bird's legal provenance.
- An Article 10 certificate, issued by the Department of the Environment, Farming and Rural Affairs (DEFRA) on behalf of the European Community. This applies only to birds of European species, or hybrids of them, and will travel with the bird for its life.
- A registration document issued by DEFRA. Currently this is renewable every three years. Only British species which are deemed 'sensitive', that is less common, require this, and such a bird should be ringed with a DEFRA ring. It is a legal requirement that you transfer the bird's registration to your name as soon as possible.

Many breeders obtain their rings from the IBR, who will issue an IBR registration form. This is optional but is increasingly common, as the majority of captive birds of prey are not of sensitive species. As with the DEFRA registration, it would be silly not to transfer your hawk to your name immediately.

RETURNING HOME

The most important thing to remember about birds of prey is that they can fly much better than you do – and the direction is often away from you!

Do not try to get the bird out of the box until you are safely indoors. Even then make sure that you are in a secure room, that is, one with a locked or bolted door. You do not want anyone popping their head round the door to inquire about your progress. You can be certain that this will happen at the exact moment that the bird suddenly makes a break for freedom.

Also make sure that the windows are fastened and, if possible, that the curtains or blinds are drawn. There are two reasons for this. In the first case the bird will remain calmer in dull lighting conditions, which will make the whole process less stressful for it, and secondly it will not hurt itself by flying against a glass window. To my shame, I once forgot these basic precautions. Fortunately the escapee was a barn owl, a native species, and there was a barn owl release scheme operating in the neighbourhood at that time!

Fitting the Equipment

If the breeder did not help you equip your bird, or you have held it in an aviary for a while, you will now have to put its various bits and pieces on it. While an experienced falconer may be able to tackle this single-handed, you will probably want someone to hold the bird so that you have both hands free. It is vital that you choose your assistant with care. Someone with a good pain threshold is best, who will not let go of the bird when it bites or foots them. Also avoid helpers with sensitive natures. If, in their inexperience, they let the bird sink something sharp into a tender part of your anatomy,

you may well question their IQ, physical appearance and their parentage. Wars have been started for less.

Holding the bird securely is essential. The bird must be comfortable and unable to get its legs or wings free (see Casting the Hawk in Chapter 4). Although it is usually recommended that the hawk should be held in a towel, with its feet against a cushion of some sort, I am against this. Use your bare hands, or soft gloves, so that you can feel the bird's body properly. Frequent handling like this is said to damage the bird's plumage. I am sure this is true, but why would you need to manhandle it regularly?

Anklets and Jesses

Anklets and jesses should be oiled and supple. You may not have spent hours sat in a corner chewing them to achieve this, but you should have worked them in your hands to soften them as much as possible. Practise fitting false aylmeri anklets to pencils or spoon handles until you can do it blindfold. If you intend using true aylmeri anklets practise using the closing tool that you will fix them with.

Make sure that you can easily insert the jesses into the anklet eyelets and attach them to the swivel. Doing this repeatedly will make them supple, and 'trains' them to go in the shape you want.

Attach the mews jesses (the pair with the slit in the ends) to the swivel. To do this pull each mews jess through the brass eyelet in the anklet until the button rest against the eyelet. Then repeat the manoeuvre on the other leg. Having done this, align the slits in the ends of both mews jesses, one on top of the other, with the suede (rough) sides against each other. They can then be treated as one piece of leather, albeit one that is twice as thick.

Pass the end of the jesses through the square (larger) end of the swivel so that the slit in them is visibly through. Take the end (with the slit) in your fingers, and bend it over the round (smaller) end of the swivel, so that this comes up through the slit. Then pull

Fastening the jesses through the swivel.

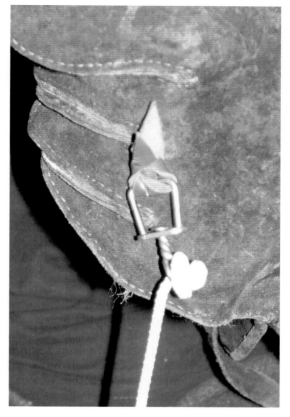

Jesses and swivel in the safety position.

the round part of the swivel through, at the same time opening the slits and working the jesses back over the square part. The jesses should be pulled as tight as possible so that they cannot loosen and slip back down the

swivel. Once this has been achieved you can then thread the leash right through the small, round end of the swivel until the knotted end is hard against it.

Because security is so important with birds of prey, at all times and not just with a new bird, you must get used to taking extreme care. At the end of a hunting day you will need to change your hawk's jesses, removing the field jesses and substituting the mews ones along with the swivel and leash. Get the slit ends of the button jesses between the fingers of your gloved hand, as soon as each is through the anklet, Only when you have them both securely held should you align one on top of the other.

Keep a firm hold of them with your gloved hand while you fasten them to the swivel. With the swivel in place, and the jesses still between your gloved fingers, it will act as a stopper should the hawk bate. Let it remain like this until you have got the leash in place.

Wind a couple of turns of leash around your free hand to prevent escape, and then pull the jesses from between your fingers. They can safely be held in the palm of your glove while you wind the leash around it a couple of times to make it secure. Only then release the leash from your ungloved hand. Unless you intend the bird to fly you must make sure that it cannot!

It all sounds very painstaking and you must be thinking I am labouring the point. Possibly so, yet every year falconers lose birds by being over-casual. One of the hallmarks of an experienced falconer is an obsession with security. It reflects how many hawks they have lost or seen lost. A cardinal sin, for a falconer, is to lose a bird of prey with its swivel and leash still attached. If you are getting your first bird make sure that carelessness does not cause its death, hung up in some distant tree by its jesses.

The Falconer's Knot

This can be tied with one hand and is normally secure, unless a hawk or falcon plays with the leash and accidentally undoes it. I know this is accidental because I had a bird that regularly did this. Having achieved freedom she would remain sitting on her perch because she thought she was still tied up. She taught me to always do a second knot for her and to pull both knots very tight.

Tying the falconer's knot requires the same obsessive attention to detail that you need when fitting the jesses. Commencing with the bird on your gloved fist, the jesses will be through the palm of your hand and the whole leash wound around your glove. The procedure is as follows:

1 Wind most of the leash off the gloved hand by wrapping it around your free hand. Stop only when there is a single turn of leash left around the glove. If you have gone too far the hawk is in no danger, as it is still secured by all the turns around your free hand. Go back a stage, if this is the case, so that the leash has the one turn around the glove and the remainder is around the free hand.

2. Approach the perch and lower the hawk down so that your glove, with the hawk still on it, is on top of the perch. This prevents the bird bating to get to the perch, something that is calculated to cause damage to its tail and wingtips. An added precaution with falcons is to make sure that your glove is put down towards the back of the block. This saves the tail catching on the block top and being bent or broken. I also find that resting my fist on the perch like this helps my balance, first thing in the morning after a heavy night – but that is a different matter.

3. Once your glove is on the perch, complete with the one turn of leash securely around it and the bird sitting happily on your fist, you can unwind the surplus leash from your free hand and get on with tying the knot. (There are different ways of describing this, and I can only use the one that I have found makes sense to most people. Instead of explaining the physical actions of the process, I find it easier to concentrate on the various visual stages – the 'what' rather than the 'how' of the thing.)

4. Pass the surplus leash down through the perch's ring so that the top part of it hangs down from the glove, while the rest of it passes through the ring and lies in a line, straight out on the floor.

5. Then take the length of leash that is on the floor and pass it around the part that is hanging down from the glove. You need to form a complete circle of leash around this, no more than 5cm (2in) in diameter.

6. Pick up some of the surplus leash (quite close to the circle you have just formed)

The falconer's knot gets easier with practice. One day you will be able to do it with your eyes closed.

and start to bring it up through the circle from underneath, as a bow. Pull this bow tight.

7. To lock the bow, insert the remaining surplus leash through it and tighten gently.

8. Repeat the knot several centimetres further up the upright piece of leash, that is, the part hanging down from the glove. If your bird proves not to be a leash worrier, and most birds are not, you may choose in future to rely on a single knot. If it does pluck at its leash you must tie the knots very tightly, or go on to the loop leash method.

With practice you should be able to tie the leash so short that, when the bird is perched, the leash just allows the ring of the perch to rest on the ground. This way the weight of the ring is not pulling on the bird's leg, yet your hawk will damage itself less when bating. The further the leash permits it to jump before it gets to the end, then the greater the jolt will be when it is brought to a halt.

A more recent innovation is the **loop leash**, which is more secure and easier to fasten.

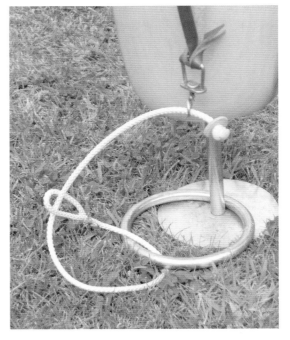

The loop leash is a safe alternative for those hawks that pick at knots.

Untying the Falconer's Knot and Picking up the Hawk

Remember about security. This is the time of greatest risk with birds of prey. Your bird is anticipating going somewhere, it has not been handled recently and is likely to bate. If at any time in this process the hawk is not attached, to either the perch or your glove, you have taken an inexcusable risk. Here is how to go about it.

Approach the perch quietly and, to avoid intimidating it, do not lean over your bird. Go in on your hands and knees if necessary. A new bird will bate furiously and will be spread-eagled on the ground as far from you as possible. It pays to be decisive at this stage. Grasp the leash in the gloved hand and slide your hand along it towards the bird, until you have hold of its jesses. Lift it clear of the ground, smoothly but as quickly as possible. This will minimize any feather damage, although the bird will probably be dangling upside down from your fist. Before touching the bird put a turn of leash around your glove so that the bird is attached firmly to your glove.

Now you can try to lift the bating hawk on to your fist, by gently using your free hand under its back. It will not try to attack you, it is much more interested in getting away. If the hawk refuses to stand on the glove, do not worry. Simply move on to the next stage with it still hanging upside down. While it is close to the perch and the ground, it can more easily damage itself. You need to get it clear of hazards as soon as possible.

Undo the two knots. To achieve this you simply unthread the surplus leash from the first turn of the knot and pull it firmly, pulling against the perch rather than the glove. The knot will disintegrate. Repeat this with the second knot. Then wind the whole of the leash securely and tightly around your glove. Do not leave it hanging in graceful loops. This may look aesthetically pleasing but it constitutes another potential hazard for your bird. Not only can the bird trap its flailing wings in the loops, with the obvious risk of damage, but the leash can more easily slip from your grasp when it is like this.

Now you can try to right your hawk, remembering to avoid threatening eye contact.

Hooding

Once the bird is safely equipped you can start training. This is the time to introduce the hood, if that is your plan. A new bird will freeze in terror (it believes that you are going to eat it, so it is anxious not to draw attention to itself) and will let you pop the hood on with a minimum of fuss. Weigh the bird and, having deducted the weight of the hood, record its starting weight.

Why Use a Hood?

When I was small I would cover my eyes with my hands or a cushion when something on the television scared me. My childish reasoning was that if I couldn't see it, then it couldn't see me.

Your hawk is terrified of all the new and strange things around it. When you hood it you have allowed it to hide and it will relax. Carrying it hooded, more or less continuously for the first couple of days, will get it used to the feel of your fist and its perch. It will accept strange sounds and can have the hood removed for brief but lengthening periods. With the hood off it will sit still on the fist for a short while until its fears build up. As it begins contemplating a bate (the headlong plunge from the glove) you can quietly slip the hood back on and calm it down again. It is a very kind thing to do.

A hawk that has been properly introduced to the hood will always be good to hood, even if it has not worn one for months. It makes visits to the veterinary surgery, or transport in busy areas, so much less stressful for it.

Accepting the Perch

At first the new bird will lie 'spread-eagled' on the ground, and then will bate furiously in an effort to escape. Only when it realizes that this is impossible will it eventually seek the highest perch available to it. This will be its block or bow, and it may take some days to learn to use it.

Carrying the Hawk

Always hold the bird on the gloved hand, with the jesses held through the palm of the hand and the leash securely wound between and around your fingers. Your hand should make a fist so that you have a firm hold of the jesses and the leash.

Hold your arm with the elbow comfortably close to the body, bending at a right angle, so that the forearm is horizontal. This last point is important, as your bird will prefer to sit on the highest place available. If you let your arm droop the bird will try to climb up your arm. This can make novice handlers lean further away from the bird, causing the arm to slope down still more and aggravating the problem. Equally, if you hold your fist high, the bird will perch on the very top, and will probably be uncomfortable and unsettled.

Keep the gloved fist fairly close to your stomach in that familiar 'pint of beer' or 'mug of coffee' position. It sounds a bit pathetic but, when I got my first kestrel, which weighed all of 180g (6oz), I was wary of its beak. In consequence I held it away from my body. I may also have had some notion that it would feel less threatened by me. The end result was that my arm soon burnt with a build-up of lactic acid. Only as I grew more confident did I start bringing my glove closer. What a difference – it had been my arm that had proved so heavy, not the bird.

Bating

Your new bird has no wish to sit on your fist. It sees you as a giant who will probably eat it. Naturally it will try to escape by hurling itself from the glove in a bate. Let it hang for a moment, until it stops flapping its wings, then gently put your free hand underneath its back and lift it back on to the glove.

The correct carrying position is comfortable for you and the bird.

Unfortunately the bird of prey, as a raptor, thinks our hands are gripping weapons like its own feet. The more you have to help it up, the more it feels threatens. You will soon learn how to flick the bird back on the glove without touching it. At this stage keep your gloved hand away from your body, possibly a little bit higher than usual, and avoid looking at the hawk. It will certainly bate again, within a matter of seconds at first. You just have to patiently repeat the process until the bates become less frequent. You will be surprised how quickly you make progress.

Feeding

How Soon Will it Eat?

This will vary with the individual. As it is starting off at a fat weight it may not eat for several days. I only start to get anxious after

Avoid eye contact with a new hawk as it can interpret this as the prelude to an attack.

four days without food. Curiously wild birds, which have known hunger, are often quicker to feed off the fist.

Helping it Feed

The more you 'man' (carry) your bird the quicker it will become used to you. Even when it is sitting fairly consistently on the glove it may still be reluctant to eat. This is not because it is not hungry, but because you offer a more immediate threat. In fact it is probably ravenous, but bending down to pull at food on the glove will involve taking its eyes off you. Sometimes the offer of titbits from your fingers will help, as it can still watch you while eating. Equally stroking its feet with pieces of meat will sometimes make it look down and pick at the food. Whatever you do it will stop eating as soon as the edge has gone off its appetite. Leaving food by its perch is counter-productive, as it will eat it but will not get any tamer. Just remember it will not starve itself to death.

Speeding Up the Manning Process

You can do this by thinking like a bird. If you stare at it you will convince it that you are

going to attack. That is exactly what it would do. So look away and let it look at you instead. Once your non-reaction becomes accepted it will feel free to look for other possible dangers. Equally avoid hand movements as it identifies our hands with its feet, which are weapons. In the wild it would not sit stroking its friends. For a start it has not got any, and secondly it would fall over if it tried.

With my first kestrel it took me ages to get it to settle on the glove for any length of time. With the wisdom of hindsight, I can see that I made things as hard for it and me as possible. I was so entranced with it that I spent all my time gazing at it adoringly. To the bird's mind this simply appeared to be the prelude to an attack, so very sensibly it threw itself off the glove in an attempt to escape. Having failed to achieve this it was then grabbed by a hand (a weapon in its mind) and once more submitted to the intense gaze. A cat playing with a mouse could hardly have been more cruel, and I am ashamed now of what I put it through.

As soon as your hawk has accepted your passive behaviour you can start being more

Facial contact is a good way to offer friendship. All birds of prey interact with their faces, so they do not feel threatened by this approach.

pro-active. Begin to look past or over the bird. It thinks you have the same range of vision as itself (about 280 degrees), so it knows that you must have seen it, yet your lack of interest will reassure it that it is not on your menu. Pretty soon you will be able to look at it directly. Begin gentle hand movements away from the bird. As it gains confidence you can move them closer and more quickly.

Birds are very aware of body language. Try to be relaxed in both your movements and your stance. You may have to slow your breathing down and consciously relax your muscles. Make your movements casual and languid.

Your bird will also respond to your tone of voice. Although you will normally be pretty silent at this stage of affairs, you may have to reply to others. Use low, comforting tones. While birds of prey are not the greatest of vocalists they do have a range of 'speech'. You would have to be a very insensitive falconer not to recognize the peremptory warning cheep when danger is perceived, the reassuring notes of a mother with her eyasses or the social tones your bird will talk to you in.

Behave like a friendly hawk. They do not attack with their beaks but use their faces when they wish to be friendly. They beak rub, food pass and preen each other. Try presenting the top of your head towards its face. No hawk would ever do this if it had any hostile intentions. This way your bird is not being stared at and, in the unlikely event of it trying to foot or bite you, it is unable to do you any harm. Depending on the bird you should eventually be able to nuzzle and kiss it.

Carrying the Hawk About

So far everything has been done while you are standing still. Very quickly your new hawk will accept this. When it seems quite at home on your fist, and is not bating at five-minute intervals, it is time to start walking about, very quietly, in the back garden. It will learn that this strange tree can move, and that this movement does not threaten it. Once you have achieved this you can start manning it in the street – at increasingly busy times of day.

As with all animal training it is best to avoid problems. Only progress if your bird has shown that it can cope with all that it has been exposed to so far. In busier and noisier conditions you can help it by turning your body to shield it from scary sights (such as heavy traffic or bicycles). This will convince it that your hand is an intelligent perch that will keep it safe. The more you carry your bird the sooner it will become relaxed enough to respond to your training.

Manning never stops. When I was first learning the sport I was lucky to know an old falconer, Laurent de Bastyai, who was endlessly patient with novices. During my many visits to his home, I do not think I ever saw him without his favourite lanneret on his fist. It was the only bird of prey I have ever seen that would eat seed cake!

To illustrate the value of manning I would like to tell you about my first Harris hawk. He was frankly terrified of heavy vehicles. I spent endless hours walking the streets around my home, to get him used to all sorts of traffic. If a bus or lorry came along I would turn to shield him from the sight, or would even walk up someone's drive to avoid a particularly noisy vehicle.

We had been together for about three weeks and I was flying him along the edge of a local wood. The hawk was behaving well, and would fly some 20 or 30m ahead before perching in a tree. I would follow, beating any likely cover towards him as I walked. Once I was up to him he would loop ahead again, and so on. At the top end of the wood he flew around the corner and out of sight. I heard a motor start up and, on my arrival, found a combine harvester and, unsurprisingly, no bird.

I got him back without too much difficulty and no harm was done. But over the years I took that bird everywhere with me. He travelled the country in the back of my car, and when I started doing displays he happily accepted marching bands, motorcycle display teams, medieval battles and so forth. He was at home on a film set, in a TV studio or on a windswept hill. In short he became Mr Cool.

One day a friend of mine was using him in a display in gale force conditions. To her horror the bird simply got blown away and was lost.

Hawks react to visual threats so shielding the hawk from traffic during manning will help it to stay relaxed.

It took us three long days to find him again, and when we did locate him he was hunting off the top of a combine harvester!

So you can never do too much manning. The more relaxed your bird is in every conceivable situation, the less likely it will be to panic and get lost. Remember too that this will apply just as much to older birds, and will need doing after every moult. The good thing is that manning takes much less effort the second time around.

Selecting a 'Classroom'

Once you are carrying your hawk freely about, and it appears relaxed in most circumstances, it is time to choose where you will do the bulk of your training. For all birds of prey you will want an area that is free from interruption and is very open. Trees of any size, even bushes, are a nuisance. They seem to exercise an irresistible attraction for any bird that is still working on a creance (the training line). Having to untangle your hawk, from the cat's cradle it has woven in the treetops is guaranteed to set your training back by days.

Even when your hawk is coming to you promptly it can get snagged up. Choose an open space with mown grass. Pastures may be suitable and quiet but they have docks, nettles and thistles sticking up, all of which can catch on the line. As the bird flies towards you it will drag a loop of line behind it through the grass. A light bird may well be stopped in its

tracks, and even a heavier one will find it requires quite an effort to get to you. If your bird is not determined it may just give up – a very undesirable lesson for it to learn.

My own choice would be a school playing field or sports ground. You can be confident that these will be empty at predictable times. An offer to take the hawk into school once it is trained will usually ensure that permission is readily given.

Your last target before starting work on the creance will be to habituate your hawk to being fed in its classroom, so that it will associate both time and place with food. Then you will be ready for the next stage.

CHAPTER 6

Early Training

Never forget that birds of prey can fly much better than you do – and have no need to come back.

CREATING A REFLEX

You do not need to teach your bird to fly – it already knows how to do that. Getting it to come back is the important bit. Training is a matter of conditioning it to respond in the same way to the same visual and audible signals, for a reward, in any circumstances. This is called a conditioned reflex and it is the basis of all animal training. It is achieved by endless repetitions.

You must be consistent yourself. Failure to give an appropriate reward each time the bird obeys will undermine its motivation to come to you. Equally, the use of erratic signals will cause confusion and the hawk may become unsure, so that it may not recognize what you want it to do.

Sometimes unexpected distractions can conspire to interfere with the working of this reflex. There may be a loud noise, the arrival of someone new, a loose dog or a hundred other things. When anything like this occurs, it is said to have inhibited the working of the reflex. Because you will eventually be flying your bird of prey in environments over which you have no control, you should welcome these interruptions as training aids. In overcoming these incidental problems, so that the bird continues to respond properly in spite

of them, you are said to have reinforced the working of the reflex against the inhibition. If you consider the many distractions that exist at an outdoor event like a county show, you will appreciate just how much the trained falcon or hawk can put up with.

SIGNALS

The visual signal will differ according to the type of raptor you are intending to train. For those hawks, buteos and owls that will be flown to the fist, the signal is an outstretched arm, which is basically no more than a substitute branch.

To make yourself as attractive as possible, you should stand sideways on to the hawk, with your gloved hand extended out horizontally at right angles to the bird's path of flight. Even from a distance this 'railway signal' shape is clearly identifiable.

The back of the glove should always be presented towards the bird. Although it can only see a tiny morsel of food, it may be fooled into hoping that this is actually the 'tip of an iceberg', and that a larger lump is hidden within your palm. In addition you will find it easier to get hold of the bird's jesses when it alights on your hand. After it has landed, and your arm is back into the normal carrying position, your hawk will automatically be facing you on the glove.

When a bird is slow to come, it is natural to extend your arm towards it. By shortening the

Calling a hawk to the fist. The outstretched arm is a clear visual signal and represents an attractive and familiar perch.

distance between you without moving your feet, you hope to make the reward appear more tempting. In fact this creates a foreshortening effect and reduces the power of the signal, making the arm look smaller and less attractive. Remember that birds of prey choose to land on the sideways branches of trees that are clearly visible. The best advice is to keep your gloved hand extended sideways. It will look bigger and the hawk is more likely to want to come to it.

With any of the falcons, and I would urge you to do this with the small accipiters as well, the signal is a swung lure. This attracts them because, as bird catchers, they are naturally drawn to any movement in the sky. Falcons especially will come in too quickly, and hit their prey too hard, to land comfortably on a glove. With the accipiters I recommend the lure because I find it is the easiest way to get them back in the hunting field. After an unsuccessful hunt, they can 'switch off' and ignore all your blandishments to come down from whatever high perch they have found. To some extent this is a natural reaction, to allow their body to recover from their efforts. A morsel of food is viewed with total disdain, but a swung lure is irresistible.

I find it quite easy to get both falcons and accipiters to come short distances to the fist once they have got used to being picked up off the lure. But the lure will always remain the preferred signal. All types of trained birds will quickly learn other signals, such as the dog going on point or the ferret box being taken off your shoulder.

The audible signal will preferably be a whistle (because it carries further) or a shout. It will be indispensable when your bird is out of sight, perhaps in a wooded area. If you cannot whistle with your own lips, you will need to buy a whistle. There are silent dog whistles on the market but I would advise against these because you cannot tell if they are working. Furthermore it is important to buy a matching spare at the same time, and you can only do this if you can hear the actual tone of your whistle. You need to do this to ensure you will be able to give an identical signal if your other whistle is out of action for any reason. The spare, in the drawer at home, is effectively the master copy, enabling you to get yet another matching replacement at any time. Remember that a changed signal can confuse your bird.

When to Introduce Signals

The first time you try to pick your bird up from its perch you will be using both visual and audible signals. By standing to the side of the bird as it faces you, your gloved hand should be extended across its chest, with the back of the glove towards it. With every species, except Harris hawks (I will deal with them separately), you should offer a small piece of food on your glove. At the same time

Pushing against its chest will make the hawk step up on to your glove.

give the familiar whistle you will always use in future. You may have to push gently against its chest to make it step up.

Falcons

The same procedure is used to lift falcons from their blocks but you will want to introduce the lure as soon as possible. To teach it to associate this with food simply swing the baited lure as you approach the block and drop it down, with your usual whistle or a shout, within range of the falcon. It will happily flutter down on to the lure. The first couple of times it may land on the ground half a metre short of the lure, and will walk up to it. If it is not very positive in its approach you can gently tweak the lure line so that it takes a firmer hold of its 'victim'. Provided you have tied the garnish of food securely to the body of the lure, the falcon will have to grip to pull its reward apart. Always wait until it is settled before making any attempt to approach, or you will sow seeds of doubt about you that will take extra time and effort to remove.

While it is eating you can carefully 'make in' to it, so that you are only centimetres away

The falcon will happily flutter a metre or two to the lure.

Going upwind to call the bird will be best as it is already looking at you.

by the time it has finished the food. At this point offer it more food on your glove, and it should step up happily. Do not worry if it keeps hold of the lure for a while. It will eventually let it drop and will switch its attention to the reward you are offering. With time a falcon that does not perceive you as a threat to its food will happily hop up on to the glove, with its lure or a kill still in its feet.

Harris Hawks

The Harris hawk is unique because it is the only bird of prey that lives and hunts in family groups. It remains with its parents for up to two years. This means that it understands co-operation and likes company. The effect this has on training is that, *at any time in its first two years*, it can imprint on you. It will also need little encouragement to learn to step to

the fist. Your problem with a young Harris is not to tame it but to prevent it imprinting. However, this is not always the case. Sometimes immature Harris hawks that have remained with their parents for a very long time are much more similar to accipiters in their behaviour and will need to be treated in the same way.

The less your Harris associates you with food the better. Therefore, the sooner it is hunting for itself, the less likely it will be to treat you as a surrogate parent. After its daily creance training, it is customary to follow the session with a period of manning. To prevent it associating your approach with a reward, you should reverse the usual sequence, and man the bird for some time before commencing your daily, food-related, training session. It is advisable just to pick it up from its perch without using food to teach it to step up. Apart from the titbits you use for training, let it find the balance of its food beside its perch, or in its travelling box, rather than giving it yourself on the glove. There is no guarantee that your Harris hawk will not scream.

THE CREANCE

Once your bird is hopping readily from its bow perch to your fist, or is dropping promptly on to the lure beside its block, it is time to introduce the creance. This light but strong line will enable you to test your hawk's response (and your training) over longer distances, but without any risk of losing it. Success is built on a progression of good experiences and it is better to make haste slowly than to rush things. Setting too high a target for each lesson may result in mistakes being made, each of which can cause the bird to lose confidence.

Although your bird is only going to come a very short distance at first, you should get into the habit of checking the wind direction before each session. Your hawk will always choose to face into the breeze so that its feathers do not lift up or get ruffled. By going upwind from it you can be confident that it will at least be looking in your direction. Just as your holiday plane takes off into the wind, so too does your bird. The wind in its face will give it instant lift and buoyancy, so coming to you will be more inviting. That same headwind will give it control, and it will be happier not to be rushed towards you. Landing on the fist will also be a much more comfortable affair.

Consider the problems your hawk will have if you neglect this basic courtesy, and ask it to come downwind. For a start it will be facing the wrong way, so you may find it hard to get its attention. It will be unwilling to turn round to face you as the wind will blow it off balance. It knows that, if it does take off, the following wind will suck all the lift away from

it. The only way to avoid this will be to launch itself towards you at a sufficiently fast pace to overtake the wind, but this will mean that it will be coming towards you at an uncomfortably fast speed. In the early days of its training it may not have the confidence to approach you so quickly and may simply fly straight past you. Even if it does make a determined attempt to come to you, it may have trouble stopping when it does reach the glove.

Tying on the Creance

Remembering the most important thing about birds of prey (that they fly much better than you), you must make sure that the bird's leash is kept wound around your gloved hand, except for the very last few centimetres. These are placed alongside the end of the creance line and the two, treated as a single strand, are

Tie the creance to the leash with an ordinary half-hitch but make sure it is secure. If in doubt tie extra knots.

tied into an ordinary half hitch. Pull them apart and they simply tighten up further. If you are in any doubt, get someone to check your knots or tie lots of them. Do not practise your knots for the first time while holding an untrained bird.

Extend the creance away from the rail or bench that you are going to fly your bird from, placing the creance handle on the ground. A few metres is sufficient at this stage. Still retaining the creance line in your hand, you can unwind the leash from your glove and put the bird on its 'launching pad'.

First Steps

Retrace your steps no more than a metre or two along the line, standing on it for security, and give the normal signals. The bird should happily come a wing flap or two to the fist, or flutter a couple of metres on to the lure. On the first day it is worth giving a sizeable reward, even though the bird will lose its appetite quickly. Approach falcons very tactfully, advancing only as the head goes down to pull at the food and stopping every time it looks up. As it finishes the bait on the lure you can offer it another reward on your glove, and it should step up.

You maybe able to repeat this once or twice, over the same short distance, until you have given all the day's ration. No matter how many or how few repetitions you do, remember always to have a secure hold of the bird's jesses and leash when it is on the fist. As you walk back to your intended distance keep the creance line in your hand. Once it is on the rail or bench, remember to keep standing on the line until the bird has come and you have a secure hold of it again.

Making Progress

Each day the bird should become more confident. Provided you keep it at its best weight it will willingly cover a greater distance the next day, repeating the flight an increasing number of times as it proves more responsive to smaller rewards. Be careful to let

The hawk will quickly fly a couple of metres to you; you can increase the distance as it gains confidence.

Advance only as the falcon pulls at the lure. Each time it looks up it is wary of potential danger so you must have checked your approach.

the bird eat what it has come for, whether off the fist or the lure. Do not pull the food away, or the bird will start snatching at your hand or, in the case of falcons, will try to carry the lure away.

As a rule of thumb I would suggest that you ask the bird to come no more than 2m (6ft)

Plucking up the courage to cross the great divide can sometimes take a ridiculous time, but you will face greater tests of your patience in future.

on the first day. If all has gone well it is reasonable to expect, if it weighs the same the following day, that it will come double that distance. Subsequently you should be able to increase the distance by 4 or 5m (13 or 16ft) a day until you are at the end of the creance. In theory it will only take eight or nine days to get your hawk to the point of free flight. In practice you will have a few setbacks, and will probably be over-cautious about taking the final step. Including manning, an experienced falconer will probably get most birds of prey flying free within a matter of three weeks. However it is not a race, so take as long as you think you need.

Problems

Of the various wrong responses the worst is probably when the bird tries to fly away from you immediately. If this happens it is obviously not manned sufficiently or is not hungry enough (or both). Since it is securely held by the creance you will be able to have another try, but you must do your groundwork better before your next attempt.

Very often, because you are being careful not to reduce your hawk's weight too

dramatically, it will refuse to come at all. It may sit on the rail and display absolutely no interest in the food. If this behaviour persists for more than a couple of minutes you can safely assume that it is not hungry enough. Do not feed it but put it back on its perch and try again later in the day, or the following day if this is not possible.

Less disheartening is the bird that shows every sign of wanting the food but cannot pluck up the courage to actually jump to your fist or the lure. It will lean forward to the very point of its balance, craning its head towards the reward. It may even flap its wings and shuffle about anxiously, and is visibly trying to steel itself to cross the great divide. You are so nearly there that it is worth persevering a little. Try getting closer so that it can almost reach the food. Once the ice is broken and it has made the decision, it will quickly start to come the distance that you first hoped for. However, the fact remains that it still needs more manning, and to lose a tiny bit more weight.

I have had the experience of trying to train an older buzzard that had never been flown free. Despite being very steady on the glove,

91

and so hungry that I feared for its wellbeing, it just refused to leave its bow perch. Only when I placed it on an unfamiliar rail did it deign to come. Having started to respond it was immediately willing to come any distance I asked, and in fact I flew it free that same day. Its problem was that it expected to be brought up short by its leash and so thought it could not fly. I have seen this since, although to a lesser degree. For this reason I prefer to use a different perch from the bird's own for doing creance work.

At the other end of the spectrum is the bird that sets off for the glove or lure before you are ready. This is not a bad problem to have but it does signify that the bird is too keen, which you must interpret as being over-hungry. It will be easy enough to remedy this by giving it a slightly larger ration. You will also have learned the bottom end of the weight range at which you can work it, which is very useful information to have.

WEIGHT AND FEEDING

Initially your young bird, fresh from the aviary, will be fat. Probably it will not eat for about four days, but you should still weigh it if it will sit on the scales. By the time it condescends to eat on the fist it will have reduced quite a lot. The weight at which it starts to eat on the glove is a pretty good indicator of its first training weight. At this weight you should be able to pick it up fairly easily for a morsel of food.

When you go to pick it up it should look interested, and should step on to your glove readily. If it does this it is close to a good weight. If it shows no interest and you have to push the glove against it to make it step up, it is too heavy. It will also be reluctant to cover its previous distance to you. In contrast, if your bird of prey is too hungry, it will be eager to get to you, bating furiously at your approach and setting off along the creance before you have got the food or lure out. The optimum weight is somewhere in the middle.

Always record the bird's daily weight, the time it was flown (try to be consistent about this in the early stages), how well it worked and how much food it was given. Over a surprisingly short time you will establish a regime that works for it.

Food Quantity

This will depend on the species and size of your bird, and on its metabolic rate. It will also vary with the quality of the food. This is why I recommend day-old chicks as the preferred diet at this stage: they have a constant value and can be counted, making it easier for you to monitor how much food you are giving.

Accipiters will normally burn up calories faster than falcons. Falcons, in turn, are likely to need a proportionately higher level of food intake than the more sedentary buteos. The only reliable measure is that which the scales dictate. If your bird remains constantly responsive while maintaining the same body-weight, you have found a pretty good level of feeding. If it becomes more responsive, to the point of being over-eager, and its weight drops the slightest amount, you need to increase its daily ration.

More usually, because we all fear that we will starve our new hawk, one day it will show a reduced desire to come for food *and* its weight will have edged up marginally. You will need to be a little meaner.

The most dangerous scenario is when the hawk shows a reduced response but its weight has not gone up. This can indicate that it is much too low in condition and is basically anorexic. Do not hesitate to feed it up very promptly, restore it to a higher weight, and start again in a few days time. You cannot do this with a dead bird!

Daily Rations

In the short term you should discipline yourself and your bird to a fairly strict regime for at least two weeks. However, a bird kept continuously at a low weight is chronically

BIRD RECORD SHEET

Bird Name: ......*Cleo*............................... Species: .....*Harris Hawk*.. Sex: ..*F*...... Hatched: ..*17/4/96*..........

Ring no/s: .... Microchip No : .... Sire No: .... Dam No: ....

DAILY FLYING AND FEEDING RECORD

Date	Weight	Start	Finish	Performance		Quarry taken	Food
3/10/04	2-4½	09·30	16·40	V. obedient, followed well in wind		2 rabbits	Rabbit leg
Weather conditions:				Cold, windy, sunny	Venue: Hill Farm		
4/10/04	2-5	09.45	12·15	Little slow to follow, chased well, no luck		0	3 chicks
Weather conditions:				Windy + grey, light drizzle	Venue: Hill Farm		
5/10/04	2-5	11-20	14-45	followed well in woods, took pheasant in brambles		pheasant	3 rabbit leg
Weather conditions:				Overcast, showers.	Venue: Grove Woods		
6/10/04	2-4¾	10·15	13-45	V sharp, chasing well, obedient, finally got soaked in pond.		Rabbit + moorhen	3 rabbit leg
Weather conditions:				Cloudy, light wind	Venue: Hill Farm		
7/10/04	2-4½	14-00	16·30	Working close to dog + took 2 pheasants + lots of chases. Also squirrel but came down with it. Not bitten		2 pheasants, squirrel	Gorged.
Weather conditions:				Mild, breezy.	Venue: Grove Woods		
8/10/04	2-7½	NOT	FLOWN				NOT FED
Weather conditions:					Venue:		

TO DO

1. Check birds feet for cuts, bites, abrasions (includes checking under anklets). Wash with mild salt solution.

2. Dry bird before putting away if wet. Particular attention to the wing buts.

3. Check all equipment is in good order for next use. Oil jesses, replace cracked bells, worn bewits, renew knot on leash if getting worn.

4. Check telemetry is still working. Discard batteries if used several times.

5. Complete Daily Record Sheet.

Always record the daily progress. It is a vital task in establishing your hawk's best flying weight.

underfed and will benefit from the occasional gorge. This is when you give the bird as much food as it will stuff in at any one time. Gorging the bird will enable it to recharge its batteries and restores its energy levels if they have become depleted. Harden yourself to withholding its food the next day. The day after that it should work well and be at the same or a marginally heavier weight than before the gorge. When at a hunting weight a bird will benefit from being gorged once a week.

A bird will benefit from an occasional gorge. Birds are kept chronically hungry during the hunting season and need to replenish their energy levels and reserves from time to time.

For small falcons and accipiters there are other considerations. Their fast metabolism may make it sensible to give a small 'buffer' meal in the morning to avoid sudden and potentially fatal weight loss. You need to be consistent and use your common sense with small raptors or it will end in tears.

Of all the small raptors the kestrel is probably the species that suffers most from beginners' ignorance. Too often they are thought of as a suitable subject for a child to learn with, and in many ways that is true. However, they are as vulnerable as any other tiny bird of prey to weight loss. I think it is important to recognize this is, and have therefore given some appropriate advice regarding their training (*see* box on p.96).

FLYING FREE

If your hawk is repeatedly coming promptly to your fist or the lure over the full length of the creance, it is time to fly it free. Birds are rarely lost the first time you fly them free (probably at a weight close to the original training weight). Disasters occur once you have become over-confident, and when you start pushing the bird's weight up.

Before You Start

Falcons are not designed to take game on the ground and they will soon be coming towards you too quickly to stop. Once they are coming about 10m (32ft) the lure needs to be offered in the air. At first they will lack the skill to catch this while it is moving, so simply dangle it at arm's length. Let them catch it and land. Before long they will be coming further and you may have time to give the lure a single swing, so that it crosses their path as they arrive. They will sometimes miss, and will either be brought to an abrupt halt by the creance or will turn smartly back to get the lure on the ground. Only when it shows this latter reaction can you release the bird with confidence. When you do, choose a dull day with little wind and fly later than your usual

time. Put on telemetry!

Any falconer, not just novices, will have a nasty moment if their new falcon appears to ignore the lure on its first free flight. Even though you think you have chosen a really open site with good visibility, it is a racing certainty that the bird will vanish behind the one roof or distant tree, which you believed was totally unimportant. Before you start to panic remember that the bird has no idea where it is. This works in your favour. No young bird, on leaving the nest for the first time, will set off in a straight line. It will instinctively go in circles, slowly expanding its knowledge of the local terrain. Your bird is no different. It will tend to come back into sight and, if you can see it, there is no doubt that it can see you and, more importantly, the lure. So hold your nerve and wait for it to

Teach the falcon to take the lure in the air. This stops it hitting the lure too hard and hurting its feet, and is useful if the ground cover would hide a dropped lure.

reappear. Sometimes it will perch somewhere, but it will not have gone far and will probably turn up within a few minutes.

If you are unlucky enough to lose your bird on its maiden voyage, bear in mind that it has not deliberately tried to escape. It has simply got lost. The chances are that it is sitting not far away, wondering where on earth you have gone. However, the bird of prey thinks rather like the Red Indian who believed that 'Indian not lost, wigwam lost': it knows exactly where it is, it is just that everything else is missing. Therefore, although it will not come looking for you, you can bet it will be mightily relieved when you manage to find it.

It is vital that you teach your falcon to catch the lure in the air. If you are trying to

Offering a dangled lure gives a young falcon an easy target to learn its footing skills.

As the falcon becomes more confident you can swing the lure into the its path so that it learns to take a moving target.

Training Kestrels

I think a lot of falconry books have served kestrels badly, in that the advice on weight control and feeding is written by experts who are used to preparing large falcons for the grouse moors. For them training is something of a race against time, to get their eyass falcons in the air as soon as possible before the young grouse become strong on the wing. The birds they are dealing with are larger and more robust, so the boundaries of weight control are nothing like as critical. It is no use saying 'if the falcon is not responding, reduce its daily food ration accordingly' when dealing with a novice and a kestrel. The beginner is not under any compulsion to get their kestrel up and flying as quickly as they dare. He or she is much more concerned with not killing or losing their pet.

With a kestrel the difference between having a bird that is so fat that it flies away, and one that is so thin that it dies, may be little more than 30g, or an ounce. Weight reduction is not, therefore, a thing to plunge into recklessly. As the sexes may be difficult to establish, until you have discovered a proper flying weight, it is wisest to assume that your kestrel should be anywhere between 170g and 250g (6–9oz) in weight. I can safely say that a daily ration of two chicks is sufficient for any male or female kestrel.

On this ration the kestrel will almost certainly show no interest in flying to you. So in your training record you can put down '14 chicks in the first week, no response, weight unaltered'. This does not matter. Keep manning the little falcon and getting it increasingly tame. Instead of reducing the weight on a daily basis I think it is a good idea to do this on a weekly one. Therefore, in the second week give it only one chick on a couple of days (say the Tuesday and Friday). I suspect that the second week's report will read '12 chicks, no response, weight unaltered'.

On successive weeks, knock one chick a week out of the bird's ration. Eventually you will find it showing an interest in coming for food. Perhaps the entry for this week will be '9 chicks, hopped 15cm (6in) to fist, weight down by 7g to 250g (a quarter of an ounce to 9oz)'. You have found a regime that is insufficient for the bird's needs, because it has lost a tiny bit of weight. Recognize that it cannot be kept healthy on this inadequate ration. So the next week increase the amount by a chick. Ideally you should now be able to write down '10 chicks, still coming a short distance once or twice, weight remained the same'. You now have a maintenance diet for the kestrel that you know it will keep healthy on.

The following week you should revert to the ration which reduced the bird's weight. Hope for '9 chicks, much keener, weight down by a further 7g to 243g (quarter of an ounce to 8.75)'. Again, go back then to the maintenance ration of 10 chicks, to achieve the next weekly report '10 chicks, still coming well, weight 243g (8.75oz)'. What you are doing is slowly edging the weight down without having to measure a daily reduction in food. Every time you achieve a drop in weight you are feeding too little, which you need to do, but you must try to stabilize this weight loss by returning to the maintenance ration on alternate weeks. This prevents the kestrel being progressively starved.

Incidentally the above regime might be appropriate for a female kestrel but would probably be too generous for a male. Each individual may vary, so follow the principle but watch and weigh the bird.

Everybody who flies a kestrel nurses an ambition to get it to hover, at a reasonable height, above them. This is difficult to achieve because hovering burns up a lot of energy and is only done to locate food. In captivity the kestrel knows exactly where the food is, so it can see no purpose in needlessly wasting energy.

The kestrel is a true falcon and, like its larger cousins, hunts for its prey from the air. However, it tends to concentrate on small mammals, and even insects, in preference to flying game. Although it can take small birds in flight these form only a tiny part of its diet (American kestrels are much more bird orientated and should be trained as a traditional falcon). This means that kestrels do not 'switch on' to the lure as readily, and in fact many are flown wholly to the fist. They can do this because they have longer tails than other falcons to help them balance when hovering, and these serve as better brakes.

In my experience I find that whatever signal is first used for a kestrel will remain its preferred one for life. For this reason I always start training them to a lure. However a lure-trained kestrel will soon learn to sit and wait for its food rather than pursuing a swung lure. They do not like to sustain flight after other birds. So, as soon as my kestrel is coming readily to a dropped lure, I abandon this and revert to flying them to the fist.

Now you can start flicking the meat in the air as the kestrel approaches. It will be a little uncertain, but will soon learn to catch tiny morsels while on the wing. Sometimes it will miss, usually because the food got stuck to your fingers or you threw it inaccurately. It begins to come towards you with less speed so that it can check its flight to drop down on these bits of food. As you both become more proficient the food can be thrown higher, so

Teaching a kestrel to stall for thrown food gets it used to hovering above you for rewards.

that it learns to stall up above you to catch the food. Once it starts doing this you can hesitate before throwing up the reward. Instinctively it will do a little hover, looking for food exactly as it would do in the wild. When it fails to catch properly on the wing (or you fail to throw the food high enough) it will learn to stoop down, as it would on a mouse in the grass.

This behaviour can be developed to the point where the kestrel starts hovering above you to bully you for food. It will become more independent if you push its weight up a little, but will also hover at a higher level. In each training session it will need only a few rewards to take the edge off its appetite, and you could be in danger of losing it. This is where your early lure training comes in. As soon as you feel its interest is waning, you can produce the lure and let it finish the balance of its daily ration on this.

I have found this is beneficial because, by working the kestrel for food that is thrown up in the air, you are encouraging it to carry its 'quarry'. It will quickly develop the habit of taking this off to eat on nearby roofs or trees. However, the sight of the lure will bring it back straight away, often performing an impressive stoop in the process.

get it back and you are standing in heather, bracken or any sort of growing crops, it will be useless to throw the lure on the ground.

Free Flying Training

Once it is flying free your hawk will be nearly ready to hunt, but you must be confident that it is prepared to come to you from higher perches; use the goal posts of your playing field to test this. This is very necessary if you are going to be hunting anywhere that is likely to have large trees, which includes the greater part of the British Isles. It is surprising how a previously obedient hawk suddenly develops an independent streak when sitting high up in a tree. It may also appear to find it quite impossible to solve the logistical problem of coming to you if there is the tiniest twig or leaf in the way.

Apart from this it will need to learn to fly in different wind directions. This should be done in gentle breezes to start with. Coming into a strong wind can test the determination of a young bird, and will certainly increase its fitness. Equally it will have to learn to land in trees on windy days. When swept along downwind, many young hawks find to their horror that trees positively jump out in front of them. They end up plastered against a mass of leaves and twigs, often hanging on grimly, upside down, to some quite unsuitable sprig of greenery.

A further test of the depth of its training is to fly it in a variety of different venues. If it responds promptly in these you have done a good job. However, the sooner it learns to hunt the better, and every free flight is a potential chase. It is just that you should be realistic if it fails to connect when conditions are less than perfect and it is still inexperienced and unfit.

Fitness is more of an issue with longwings that are to be entered to game. The falcon has no chance of avoiding the wind conditions and, whatever these may be at ground level, you can bet they will be much stronger 100m (300ft) up. Here you will find yourself caught

Your hawk must come from higher perches. It is surprising how a few metres of elevation can suddenly encourage disobedience.

gain height but will soon swing downwind and find that all its lift has suddenly disappeared. Turning back towards you, and coming into the wind, it will once again hit the updraught and gain that delicious lift. Before very long it will begin to work along the ridge, going left and right and facing continually into the wind. It is doing this for pleasure but, coincidentally, will be doing this where you are. You can confidently let it get quite high before getting out the lure.

You will not need to work it to the lure as the wind has already exercised it sufficiently. Your falcon is getting fit, it is developing a taste for climbing, and it is learning that the lure is an easy and available meal. Moreover, it is coming to the lure from a height and, if you can stage-manage things so that it is coming with the wind behind it as well, it will develop the habit of stooping downwind. As it gains confidence you should only produce the lure when it is more or less above you. It will begin to anticipate this and will start to come over you to bully you for the lure. This is the basis for waiting on.

You can develop this even further by walking along the ridge. The falcon will start to keep an eye on what you are doing, which can be most useful in the hunting field. If your bird will wait on patiently, even when the dog has made a false point, you may be able to leave it up there for a while in case the dog connects with another covey.

Exercising a falcon to the lure, as you will have seen in demonstrations, is rewarding to do and will build up your falcon's fitness and footing skills. If done too much, at too early a stage, it can also result in the falcon becoming lure-bound. This is when it becomes so besotted with the lure as its preferred quarry that it ignores proper game. Because it knows where its quarry is, it has no need or desire to gain the height that is essential to a hunting falcon. Without learning this it cannot stoop effectively, and will only get involved in tail chases. It will be unlikely to catch game in this way and will become disheartened,

between two stools. On the one hand you want to get the falcon responding to the lure, and on the other hand you want it to go up high. The two are contradictory. While the lure is in sight the young bird will stay relatively low, but if you hide the lure to encourage it to climb higher it may rake away further than you feel comfortable with.

Like so many things with animal training, it is important to set up the ideal situation. What you want to find is a long ridge that faces squarely into the prevailing wind. From the top of this the young falcon will relish the lift that the updraught gives it. It will quickly

Problem Solving – Manning		
Fault	Cause	Remedy
Untrained bird has got free	Inadequate security	Observe proper precautions at all times
Bird fails to sit steadily on glove and continually bates.	Intimidated by handler's body language	Avoid direct eye contact and unnecessary hand movements. Adopt passive posture and introduce head/facial contact. Continue manning
	Arm/glove being held at uncomfortable angle	Carry in recommended position
	Bird is being exposed to experiences beyond its ability to cope	Man in quieter areas, or at less busy times, until bird is more confident
Bird has no interest in food	Bird is still too fat	Try again later or withhold food until next day
	Bird is too thin, despite previously eating on the glove	Feed up immediately. Start again once bird is stronger
Bird does not step up on glove.	Bird is still unsure of handler and/or is too fat	More manning, more tactful approach, less food

making it even more inclined to focus all its energies on the lure, which it knows from experience is prey that it can catch.

A falcon that flies at a low 'pitch' (or hunting height) like this can be improved by allowing it a lot of free flying time in very open areas. With constructive neglect you can encourage it to range further and higher, often at quite a high weight. When you do want it back the lure should be given immediately. This is sometimes described as 'flying at hack to the lure'.

Encouraging a Prompt Return

One of the great dilemmas for a new falconer is what to do when his or her new bird of prey suddenly refuses to come, having previously responded satisfactorily. You realize that it is not hungry enough, but have only discovered this after you have got to the intended distance for that day's lesson. You could go back and try again later but you want to progress the training somehow. If you persevere in calling it, will each unsuccessful repetition of the signal teach it to ignore you? Alternatively, you could get a quicker response by shortening the distance between

you, but is the bird then teaching you to come to it, instead of the other way round?

My personal advice is to go for a quick response, even if this means reducing the distance. I really do not want my birds to question whether they have to come or not. The reflex I am trying to condition into them is that the signals mean 'Come immediately', not 'Come when you like.'

If it is any consolation to anyone struggling with an apparently wilful hawk, I must confess that my own birds do not always respond as quickly as they should. Invariably this is because I have hoped that they will be obedient at what I know is not an ideal weight. This is totally stupid of me. Birds of prey have no concept of such a thing as generosity of spirit, nor will they do anything through a desire to please you. They are governed solely by self-interest.

Most domesticated animals are social creatures, living naturally in herds, flocks or packs. They instinctively understand social hierarchy and feel a need to gain acceptance by pleasing their pack leader. This means that abstract rewards, like praise, are sought after and appreciated. For the bird of prey, which is

Problem Solving – Creance Work		
Untrained bird has got free	Inadequate security	Observe proper precautions and practise tying creance before using it in earnest
Bird has no interest in food or lure	Bird is too fat	Try again later or withhold food until next day
	Bird is too thin despite previously eating	Feed up immediately. Start again when bird is stronger
Bird appears keen but will not leave perch	Bird is too fat	Try again later, shorten the distance, or withhold food until next day
	Bird believes it cannot leave perch	Use a different perch for creance work
	You are increasing distance too much	Be less ambitious to get a quicker response
Bird comes before you are ready	Bird is too hungry	Adjust weight by slight increase in food ration
Hawk, buteo or owl snatches food off glove and tries to fly off	Not sufficiently confident in you and possibly still a bit heavy	More manning and reduce food a little
Falcon veers away from lure and tries to fly off	As above	As above
Bird mantles over food/lure, risking damage to tail and wing feathers	Lacks confidence in you and may be too hungry	More manning, increase food ration slightly, and be more tactful while it is eating
	Bird sees you as a competitor, often as a result of imprinting and normal in Harris hawks	Never try to remove food it has got in its feet
Falcon strikes lure but does not bind to it	Coming too quickly to stop in time	Present lure in air. Hanging at first, later swung in towards its feet
Falcon mantles and tries to carry lure	Bird sees you as a competitor	Exercise great tact in approaching it on lure, and only try to pick it up when it has finished its food

primarily a solitary individual, such considerations are meaningless. Only if an action will provide an immediate, tangible reward can they be motivated to do it – and then only if they need that reward at that time. Whereas effective praise will encourage your dog to respond more readily to a command, the bird of prey, motivated only by hunger, will get increasingly less responsive with each reward it receives. Eventually it will cease to respond at all.

This lack of social structure also means that your hawk will be totally indifferent to your displeasure. There will be times when you may cheerfully wish to strangle this impossible, disobedient creature that you once had such high hopes for. You might just as well save your energy.

This does not mean that you cannot develop a relationship with your bird. I believe that, as far as they are able, they do become fond of us. It is just that it will not show in any greater reliability or obedience. Where it *does* evince itself is in the bird's willingness to come to you at a weight that would make it unresponsive to anyone else. Also your bird may become very trusting, allowing you to take liberties in handling it, cleaning its beak or feet and so on, that come from having complete confidence in you. The same bird, when flying free, may choose to come and sit beside you, and may

Holding a hawk's tail to prevent damage is particularly important with accipiters, which have quite brittle feathers

welcome you when you enter the mews. These are great compliments, but you should never rely on your relationship to guarantee obedience.

LUREWORK

Once your bird of prey is flying free you are progressing towards hunting with it. As a step along the way the use of a lure is of great value. The lure is simply a substitute for the bird's intended quarry, and should look as much like the real thing as possible. This means that a falcon or small accipiter's quarry may be garnished with the wings of rooks, duck, partridge, grouse or whatever. A dummy rabbit will be suitable for buteos and the larger accipiters that you expect to use on ground game.

The purpose of using the lure is to encourage the bird to recognize and chase the preferred quarry. You can teach it to take this on the move, familiarize it with the weight of the quarry, accustom it to remaining still when being approached on a kill and, most importantly of all, get it used to being bribed

off its victims. With falcons it can be used extensively to exercise the bird and with all raptors it can be used to encourage a prompt return.

Using the Ground Lure

Feeding a hawk or buteo with meat tied to a 'dummy bunny' can start beside the bird's bow perch. It takes little imagination to envisage the progressive stages whereby the bird is encouraged to chase and catch this substitute quarry over steadily increasing distances. When it has caught the lure you should approach tactfully and be kneeling or squatting beside the bird by the time it has finished the food. The accipiters tend to have very brittle tail feathers, and can break these if they mantle over their quarry. It is useful if your hawk will permit you to gather these together to protect them. Once it has completely devoured the food you can cover the lure with your hawking bag, a cloth or whatever you intend using. It will then be less worried about being dispossessed.

When its feet and the lure are covered you can offer it a titbit to bribe it off its 'kill'.

101

Cover the kill with your bag so that it cannot be seen. Your hawk will soon release it as there is no point in hanging on to something that is evidently not there.

Throw food to one side to bribe a hawk off the ground lure. It will much prefer a visible reward to the non-existent one in its talons.

Personally I have given up holding food out to one side on the glove as a means of achieving this. Nowadays I throw a small reward (about the size of a chick's head) to one side, so that it is clearly visible to the hawk. Realizing that it can get this without any interference, it will let go of the lure much more readily. After it has eaten this it can easily be lifted up on to the glove, and you can practise smuggling the lure into your bag, as you will have to do with a real rabbit.

Some hawks become very 'sticky-footed', that is, unwilling to release their quarry. I believe this is more a case of being unable to let go because they have gripped so hard than mental stubbornness. You need to be extremely patient with such individuals, which can be a real pain at field meetings, because no one else can fly anything until your bird has surrendered its kill. I have had two female Harris hawks with this fault, which have broken talons rather than release their hold.

As a further prelude to hunting you can start hiding the lure in bushes, or even down

Smuggle the lure into your bag before the hawk has finished its titbit or it may be back on the quarry – or your bare hand.

rabbit holes. With the help of an assistant to pull the dummy, use your beating stick to 'flush' the lure out of its hiding place, thus teaching the hawk to watch what you are doing in the hope of a rabbit emerging. Similarly you can slip the ferret down one end of a pipe while your assistant drags the lure out of the other. The bird will begin to associate human help with finding game, and you are ready for the real thing.

Using the Swung Lure

Working a falcon to a swung lure is a satisfying thing to do. It develops your bird's fitness, agility and footing skills. While the falcon (or accipiter) is on the creance you are limited to presenting the lure in the air. This will develop its footing skills and give you both practice at bribing it off. Once you have taken the plunge and flown your bird free a few times, you can move on to greater things. Instead of letting the falcon catch the lure you can pull the lure out of its reach at the last minute. Ideally the falcon should snatch at empty air and be left with the thought that, if it had gone faster, it could have caught the lure. Having missed, the falcon should bank round, perhaps gaining a little height as it turns, and power in again.

Your job is to build up a pattern of success in the falcon's mind. After a few days of letting it have one pass (the flight at the lure which was not successful) before rewarding it, you can move on to trying for a second pass. When the bird is readily doing this you can introduce a third pass. It is important that the bird always gets the lure before it gets tired. If it becomes weary it will look for a perch, and you really do not want this to happen because when a bird has landed you may be forced to tempt it off its perch by giving it the lure. This teaches the bird that perching is a rewarding, first-class hunting technique – which is not exactly what you had in mind.

As soon as the falcon is anticipating flying to the lure it is an excellent practice to let it take off and cruise around for a few minutes. This will help it develop a sense of territory, as it will look out from you instead of in at the lure all the time, and will enable it to build up stamina by flying at a more gentle pace. More importantly, it will not think of the lure as its signal to start flying but as a reward for coming back once it has developed an appetite.

Wild falcons may spend a lot of time on the wing, but most of this consists of gliding, with as little effort as possible, on air currents and thermals. Actual chasing probably consists of no more than a couple of stoops, and a few twists and turns. By then they have either caught their victim or it has escaped. To persist after a lure for prolonged periods of time is unnatural for a falcon and is learnt behaviour. The acceleration and tight turns displayed by a good lure bird are very demanding. Such a performer will be fitter than a wild bird, just as a professional athlete will be fitter than the average active person. I know this is true because, on those occasions when a wild falcon has interrupted a display to have a bit of a dust-up with one of my birds, my falcon has never been beaten for speed or stamina.

Lure Swinging Techniques

On a greyhound track the electric hare is driven to stay just ahead of the dogs so that they always think that it may be possible to catch it if they try that little bit harder. Ideally you want your bird to feel the same, but you will probably be unable to keep the lure in front of it for more than a second or two at a time. It is important to make those fleeting moments as stimulating as you can.

When you swing a lure you will find that you have most control over it when the lure line is kept short and it swings on a tight arc. Unfortunately this is when the lure is least attractive to the bird. Being unable to fly in tight circles, it will much prefer it when the lure is swinging in as straight a line as you can manage. This will be when the lure line is allowed to extend further from your body, which is when you will have the least control over it. I mention this because you will eventually have to become skilled at altering the arc of swing as the bird is flying.

Before you can aspire to those giddy heights you need to know how to perform the various manoeuvres with the lure. Do not feel you need to be too proficient. Every time the falcon catches you out will increase its confidence. In fact experienced lure swingers can run a very real risk of disheartening a young bird by continually outwitting it. Instead of staying on the wing it may take to perching until you give it an easy reward. Always remember that if the falcon hits the lure, even if it does not bind to it, you must let the lure drop to the ground. Because it believes that it can get the lure, it will be encouraged to fly really aggressively. Dropping the lure on the slightest impact will also prevent you pulling out any of the bird's talons as it foots the lure.

The Basic Lure Movement

When you swing the lure it will be rotating in a circle, parallel to the direction you are facing. For a right-handed person this will be on their right side, and on the left side for left-handed falconers. Starting from a point beside your feet it should swing forward and up. At the apex of the swing it will come back over your shoulder and dip down to its original starting position. This is a continuous movement and you should practise walking about and changing direction without interrupting the lure's smooth rotation. A lot of people become frozen to the spot, ending up cocooned in the lure line like a human maypole.

The lure handle will be in your gloved hand, with about your body's width of line between that and where you are holding it, loosely, with your free hand. You will find that you can shorten and lengthen the arc of the lure by moving your free hand along the lure line, away from or closer to your gloved hand respectively. This too is something you should practise.

The Forehand Pass

The lure will be used like a matador's cape to entice the falcon to follow it in the direction you wish. The easiest pass is the forehand pass. This will be to the left for right-handed people and vice versa for left-handers. As the bird flies at you, let the lure go forward towards it by allowing the centrifugal force to drag it through your fingers. If you now try to draw the lure in quickly it will hit your body, followed closely by the falcon. Let the latent matador in you take over. Step back a pace to one side of its line of flight, extend your arms, and pull the lure past you on a level plane.

The forehand pass.

The backhand pass.

This presents the lure in front of the bird for the maximum amount of time, and in the straightest direction. With practice you can time this so that the bird's feet strike out and just miss the lure. As the bird comes past you must turn to keep the lure ahead of it.

At the end of the lure's arc it will naturally curve away from the falcon's attack, and you can shorten the lure line by pulling it through your free hand with your gloved one. You will have turned with the bird so that you are now facing in the opposite direction. Quite possibly, if you keep the lure swinging on this horizontal plane, it will wrap itself around your body. To avoid this indignity, raise the lure line up with your free hand so that it circles higher than your head. When it is behind you, let your hand resume the position you used for the basic lure movement. With practice it will once more be circling parallel with your body, ready for the next approach and pass.

The Backhand Pass

A lot of quite experienced lure swingers are unable to do this pass. This is a pity as it allows you to change the falcon's direction and leads to a more varied display. The problem is that you need to be able to switch to swinging the lure on the 'wrong' side of your body, and back again, at will.

To achieve this you must practise. Start with the lure swinging on the normal side. As it comes up from beside your feet, move your free hand across to the opposite shoulder. The swinging lure, at the apex of its arc, will now drop over the opposite shoulder. If your free hand is far enough across, the lure can now start rotating parallel to you on this side. To return it to the orthodox position simply wait until its rotation brings it up in front of you, then move your free hand back to the usual side. With practice you can walk about as you continually change from one side to the other.

To do the backhand pass you will have the lure circling towards the bird, but on your 'wrong' side. Again, present the lure towards your falcon as it attacks by extending the line through your free hand. This time step aside and pull the lure past you in a backhand movement. The bird's speed and your momentum as you spin round to keep the lure in front of it, will leave you facing the opposite direction. Regain control of the lure and await the next approach.

Further Variations

From the basic lure swinging movement you can also elect to try an **overhead pass**. This is mechanically quite simple to do, but the timing is difficult. Instead of moving to one side as your bird zooms in, you can choose to stand your ground but extend the lure up high. If done properly it will teach the falcon to climb rapidly in pursuit of its quarry. Avoid giving your bird an uppercut with the lure. This pass can only be done when the wind is from behind you, so that the falcon can climb into this. In a following wind it will be unable to gain height and the manoeuvre will be pointless. I like this pass if I am trying to encourage a young falcon to stoop. As it climbs it will lose momentum. The lure will be directly beneath it and it has only to do a stall turn to be coming down in a short, but near vertical, stoop. Once it finds that this is a successful technique it will be more confident of stooping from increasing heights.

The way a falcon **exits a pass** can be varied according to the wind direction and the angle at which you pull the lure away. When you are flying the bird into the wind it can be made to climb by lifting the lure towards the end of its arc. Conversely, with the wind behind it, you can make it fly out further by ending the pass with a downward slant. The bird will have lost a little height and will need to fly out further to regain this.

Presenting the Lure

When you gauge that the falcon has had sufficient exercise, or has achieved the purpose of that particular lesson, you will want to reward it with the lure. Ideally this should be done in the air, by slowing down your forehand or backhand pass to allow it to catch the lure. Bring it to a gentle halt by letting the lure line be pulled through your

fingers, so that they act as a brake. Following the arc of the lure's movement your bird will come down in a circle, so that there is no jolt on the lure.

The most spectacular presentation is when the lure is thrown up high so that the falcon has to climb vertically to catch it. This is a useful exercise if you have a very quick bird, as it forces them to slow down before impact with the lure. I use a very long lure line, about 20m (65ft) of it, which I trail behind me while I am flying. It is easy to get tangled up in so much line, or to tread on it, so again you would need to practise a lot.

Luring Accipiters

Because the accipiters are extremely agile and turn in a surprisingly tight space, you will be unlikely to be able to work them to the lure as you might do with a falcon. Do not be too ambitious. Use the lure to encourage a quick return and some good footing skills.

Hazards

At one time I used to throw the lure up and let go of the stick, which enabled me to get more height. However, on occasions the falcon, having caught the lure, would turn with the wind instead of landing and be swept away. Twice the trailing lure stick hit spectators on the head, and both times the victim was very bald indeed! Fortunately both men were unhurt, and expressed pleasure at having been singled out in this way.

The greatest concern is for the bird's safety. It may be hit by the lure or may get tangled in the line. If you have swung too early it will learn to cut across the angle and catch the lure as it comes round behind you. Anytime the falcon catches a moving lure it can damage its feet and you should never try to pull the lure away. It has won, so give in gracefully.

When a falcon is pursuing a lure it is concentrating on that to the exclusion of everything else. It does not look where it is going. Make sure that you do not steer your bird towards potential danger. With a following wind it will be unable to change direction or climb. A young falcon will learn to gain height quicker after it has been spread-eagled against a mass of foliage, but more solid obstacles are dangerous. An experienced lanneret of mine died when it was swept headfirst against the trunk of a tree. It thought it had left plenty of clearance but a sudden gust blew it off course. This happened some 200m (650ft) from where I was standing, and the bird was simply flying out to regain its pitch.

Even the falconer can get hurt. I have been hit in a painful place more than once when I changed my mind about the side on which I was going to pass the falcon. Other accidents occur when the lure gets out of control and ends up festooned about your body. An over-keen falcon may well, in its enthusiasm, grab that part of your anatomy that is closest to the lure. This is fine if you are in to body piercing.

Lastly, if you practise your lure work as much as you should, you will get some very nasty blisters on the fingers of your ungloved hand.

CHAPTER 7

Hunting and Fieldcraft

WHERE TO HUNT

All of Britain is owned or managed. There is nowhere that you can hawk without permission, and without permission you are not only trespassing, you are also poaching. This is sometimes forgotten by a few over-enthusiastic falconers. A conviction for this could result in a jail sentence, a heavy fine and the confiscation of your equipment, including your bird and vehicle. Having thus obtained a criminal record you may find that employment opportunities are less, and little things like credit rating may be affected.

Be aware too that you have a wider responsibility towards the image of your sport as a whole. Today's public opinion is moulded by a sensation-driven media. Among their favourite targets, certainly in the current political climate, are field sports of all types. Bringing falconry into disrepute, through the behaviour of isolated individuals, is something we should all seek to avoid.

Crossing Land Boundaries

Provided the game was flushed where you have permission, it is legally yours, and you are entitled to enter your neighbour's land to retrieve your hawk and game. You cannot slip your bird at game on adjoining land.

Getting Hawking Land

If you do not already know any farmers or landowners you must look for land which carries a good stock of game. Drive around

your locality. For the austringer land with wooded areas and hedgerows will provide cover for all sorts of game. You may see fresh rabbit diggings in roadside banks, and further investigation will reveal extensive rabbit damage along neighbouring hedges. Hawking only needs a light population of game; indeed, the heavy densities that are found on shoots can be a positive embarrassment. This means that you can get by with less productive land.

The falconer with aspirations to hunt grouse or partridge will need access to serious acreage and, if he is to guarantee a sufficient supply of birds for his falcon, may have to pay for stocked land. This is a straightforward commercial transaction but he will be in competition with the shooting fraternity, who can almost certainly pay more. If your pocket cannot stretch to this you may be better lowering your sights and going for rook or duck hawking. Very few falconers are able to fly their falcons properly on game. Many will tell you that they do, but a week or two on a poorly stocked moor at the end of the season will consist of little more than watching their bird tail-chase distant grouse.

In many country areas you will see pheasants and partridge feeding on the fields. There may be strips of maize, kale or alfalfa planted next to woodland as game cover. Land such as this is invariably stocked for shooting and closer examination may reveal feeders and rearing pens, and other indicators of a managed shoot.

The chance of getting permission to use it will be nil. The landowner is doing this to obtain an income, and you will probably be unable to compete with the sort of money that shooting generates. On rare occasions a sporting landowner will permit you to use less productive areas of their land or may allow you to work the boundaries. While you may catch some pheasants you will effectively 'dog in' the others, that is, drive them back to the main body of the estate. In my experience only locals or personal friends are likely to get permission to do this. Syndicated shoots are notoriously jealous of every bird they put down. Theirs is a numbers game and they are unlikely to agree among themselves whether to give you permission or not.

Identifying stocked land will not, therefore, result in you being able to roam across it at will. However, there may be adjoining land that you might be allowed on which will be home to some of their neighbour's more wayward birds.

Most people start with a hawk that can catch rabbits, and farmers love to get rid of these. By the middle of summer they are sick of the sight of rabbits of all sizes grazing their crops. Ferreting with nets is impossible to do properly until after the breeding season, baby rabbits are not worth the price of a cartridge, and farmers do not want lurchers running through standing crops. A polite phone call with a follow-up visit may well result in permission.

Accumulating Land

Start by purchasing a large-scale Ordnance Survey map of your area. This will show field boundaries, streams, woods and so on. Get the landowner to mark his boundaries on your map. Then use highlighter pen to mark his land – and put his telephone number and name on. Ask your new host if he knows of anywhere else that might give you permission. Farming is often a family business and he will probably have relatives with land. With luck you will slowly turn your map pink with different parcels of land. Never refuse even the smallest plots of land. They may not be workable by themselves but one or two small, unimportant pieces of land can suddenly gain significance if they link bigger bits together. Before long you can have substantial tracts of land at your disposal.

Use your host's local knowledge to find out where you cannot go as well. Mark any hazards on your map (*see* below).

Making a Good Impression

Presentation is important. Skinheads with combat clothing, tattoos and piercings will find it harder to get hawking land than smartly dressed, clean-cut characters. Ideally you should try to establish some sort of reference on your first contact, such as 'I've been given your name by So-and-so (naming a mutual acquaintance)'. This gives you an immediate respectability and background. Even if you cannot supply a name you can still make a good impression by using a little flattery, for example 'Every time I pass your farm I am always impressed by the condition of your cattle (or how well maintained the land is), and I thought I would ask if you would mind …' If the farmer needs more convincing you can offer to bring the hawk over to show him, and perhaps take him out for half a day with it.

Reassure him of your respectability by offering to telephone before every visit. He will appreciate the courtesy, and will soon tell you not to bother. It helps if you report any damage to fences or let him know of any stock that is not well. He will probably know this already, but the fact that you are evidently responsible will make him glad to have an extra pair of trustworthy eyes about the place. Always close gates after you if they were shut when you found them, and leave any open gates open. Offer to take him or his family out with you, and make sure a bottle of his favourite tipple gets to him at Christmas.

Farmers are increasingly isolated. Do not neglect to stop and have a chat. You may be the only fresh face he will see all day. Over a period of years you may build up a close relationship. On one farm, which I have hawked for many years, I approached the farmer for leave to put in a few pheasant feeders to hold visiting birds on the land. He gave this readily, and also the grain to put in them, and fills them himself if I have not got time. A request to lay a few hawthorn trees to create little pockets of shelter for game, resulted in him disappearing, only to re-emerge with his chainsaw. In return, whenever I am at the farm, he feels free to ask me to help with any tasks that need an extra pair of hands.

Hawking Syndicates

Because of the difficulty of getting permission to hawk well-stocked land, some falconers are now forming syndicates and renting land to put down their own game. There is endless potential for disagreement if the ground rules are not clearly drawn up at the start. How many days can each member hawk the land? What happens if someone does not do their share of feeding and watering the pheasant poults? However, we may well see more syndicated hawking grounds in the future.

Unsuitable Land

You may sometimes get permission to hawk land that is not suitable. Recently I was offered access to some fields that were alive with rabbits. On a preliminary survey, when I was just congratulating myself on my good fortune, I looked over a hedge to find that the adjoining farm specialized in free-range chickens! Always check if any nearby residents keep a few hens or ducks around their gardens. Replacing them can be an expensive hobby (it is always a rare breed that your hawk has murdered), and your host will regret having been the cause of upsetting his neighbours.

More dramatically there are several man-made hazards to avoid (*see* below).

In summary you should seek permission to hawk land that carries an adequate stock of game, and that is free from hazards to others and to your bird. When you do obtain this, be very conscientious in cultivating the owner, and conducting yourself in such a way that you cannot be open to criticism.

WHEN TO HUNT

Game may only be hunted during the appropriate legal season. This varies with different species and regions, but is broadly speaking the winter. If you are in any doubt contact the local Countryside Alliance officials, or DEFRA. Vermin is not protected in the same way but you will have ethical and practical constraints (*see* below).

Know When to Stop

Novice falconers are notoriously reluctant to stop their hawk in the spring. It has probably taken them a while to get it working well, and they want to really establish its hunting skills before laying it off. Their bird has not yet dropped any feathers, signifying the start of the moult (*see* Chapter 4), and there are lots of tempting baby bunnies about.

There is an ethical problem to hawking late in the spring. It is not good practice to kill baby anythings – or their nursing mothers! Hawking late in the season will present practical difficulties as well. There will be more cover. Some of this will be on the trees, and it is a lot harder to spot a missing bird when the leaves are thickening. Also in the trees are nesting birds, which could easily present your hawk with an unexpected free meal. Try getting it back then. Young game can weigh much less and it is correspondingly easy for your hawk to carry.

Winter hawking is rarely affected by hot air thermals. From late spring onwards this can be an issue (*See* Hawking Hazards below).

HUNTING TECHNIQUES

Some people are blessed with fieldcraft as an in-built instinctive skill but many more have to learn it, and quickly. A bird that is continually presented with impossible slips will come to believe that there is no point in chasing quarry that it cannot catch. Instead it learns to rely on you as its one dependable source of food. Instead of pursuing game, even on achievable slips, it will turn aside and wait for your ever-reliable glove to produce its reward. Taking its weight down will not help – as it feels weaker it will be even less inclined to waste valuable energy on fruitless chases.

Falconry and hawking involves an unholy alliance that started in the mists of time (my theory anyhow). It is a case of mutual exploitation. We exploit the bird of prey's ability to catch things while it in turn exploits our ability to find things for it to chase. As long as we can keep pushing game out underneath it, the bird will stick around because we are useful to it. There are four basic techniques that you will use.

Self-Hunting

In the wild the young bird of prey chases all sorts of suitable and unsuitable quarry. After many misses it finally gets lucky, probably on a common species. 'Aha!' it thinks to itself, 'I have discovered the secret of life.' From then on it will pursue that species with increasing commitment, leading to more success. It may even become a specialist, feeding primarily on the one species. It is learning to find and hunt its own game.

The captive-bred bird of prey can do the same thing if allowed the freedom to experiment. This is the principle behind hacking falcons. The problem is always that the lack of contact will break down its dependency on you, and you may easily lose it.

Sometimes self-hunting starts when the bird is being flown and it sees something to chase. Once it develops this habit it will continually be scanning for victims. For the novice without a dog or ferret, a self-hunting hawk is more productive than one that is forced to rely on its owner's efforts. Unfortunately it is also

learning that you are superfluous to its efforts. Harris hawks are often entered like this because they are frequently flown free and encouraged to follow on. With birds that have become too lure-bound or glove-bound this is a worthwhile technique to practise, but only in the short term.

As any bird of prey becomes more experienced at hunting it will become more and more self-sufficient. While it will willingly use you, the dog or the ferret, it will, simultaneously, be scanning for its own game. When it bates you are virtually forced to let it go, as you have to back its judgement. In a game-rich area this means that you will be forever chasing after it. On land that it knows well you may have difficulty getting it to concentrate on the less productive places. It will always make its way to its favourite spots instead.

With the buteos and accipiters self-hunting is seldom more than an inconvenience as they do not pursue game for long distances. The longest flight that I ever had, with a Harris hawk, was measured on an Ordnance Survey map at almost three-quarters of a mile. This was from the top of an open hill, which only required the bird to glide downwards, and ended in water meadows by the river. Mostly a flight that exceeds 200m (650ft) is a very long flight.

Falcons are a different matter. If they start to self-hunt instead of waiting for you to flush game, they can, literally, go for miles. Therefore, you must never put a falcon up in the air unless you know that there are birds beneath it. A reliable pointing dog is an absolute must.

Stalking

With the honourable exception of skylark hawking with merlins this applies to hawks and buteos only. If you have good fieldcraft, plenty of game, and if you can move with the stealth of a wild animal, this is a possibility. It relies on your ability to approach game unseen from such a direction that your bird has a downwind and/or downhill slip while the quarry is forced to escape away from cover. This takes a lot of management, but does mean that the bird associates you with successful hunts. You need to have a good awareness of where game is likely to be, which direction the wind is blowing and how to avoid being seen, smelled or heard. Walking across the land with your hawk on the glove does not constitute stalking. This is just a case of aimlessly hoping that something will materialize.

Falcons need to be in the air, but to release them in the hope that you will find something for them to chase before they spot quarry of their own accord, is nothing more than a pipe dream. Putting them up and then running about like a madman in the hope of flushing game, is so stupid it is really not worth further comment. Even if you have spotted partridge or grouse at a distance, there is no guarantee that you will be able to find them after you have released your bird. You are simply inviting the bird to rake off and self-hunt.

Beating Cover for Game

Did the primitive hunter, while he was searching for anything vaguely edible, watch the wild hawks hunting above him? Did he, by design or accident, rattle the bushes with his spear so that game was flushed? If the hunting birds then caught the quarry, did he then try to steal it off them? Equally, because he disturbed the cover and flushed out quarry, did the birds keep an opportunist eye on his movements? Is modern falconry merely a more formal version of a symbiotic relationship that started so many thousands of years ago? We do not know, but you must admit it sounds feasible.

I once flushed a hunted woodpigeon out of a small larch plantation while a tiercel peregrine continued to circle overhead – waiting on as correctly as any trained falcon. It got it too. And kestrels commonly follow the farmer as he cuts his hay for the mice that are exposed. I have seen sparrowhawks

cruising alongside my truck, waiting for small birds to dart out on the other side of the hedge. Perhaps it is a rather vain of us to believe that we that started falconry.

Beating is indiscriminate and works on the assumption that there should be something there. A line of beaters, walking up game, works well with hare and skylarks (the merlin, although a falcon, is flown from the fist). It can work with rabbits if your land is really infested and they lie out in bits of rough cover. All experienced rabbit hawkers automatically swish their stick at any clump of nettles or bracken on the off-chance it will hold a bunny. Beating is probably the best way to serve sparrowhawks if you are working hedgerows.

A good knowledge of your land will enable you to know where game should be hiding. You can stand on an elevated vantage point while your beater/s work the cover towards you or, if you are alone, you can cast the bird up into a strategically well-placed tree and perform the beating yourself. Because you do not know exactly where any quarry is hiding, you run the risk of flushing it away from the hawk. However, beating is at least proactive and will be acceptable to the hawk, particularly if the land is not well-stocked and is therefore free from the temptations of self-hunting.

Beating is a great way to lose weight and keep fit. It will always be part of your armoury of skills, but you will want to move on to more efficient techniques.

Flushing

This occurs where you know exactly where the game is, and you are able to stage manage the whole endeavour. You can choose where to position your hawk to best advantage, and the direction in which to flush the game to help capitalize on this. You may be lucky enough to have spotted the quarry yourself, but this will not happen very often. It is time to call in expert help.

The dedicated falconer will hunt over a dog and/or ferrets. For anyone hunting seriously with falcons, a pointing dog is a must. It is the only way to ensure that you can serve your bird before you let it loose. The pointer or setter will quarter vast swathes of land, working into the wind in pursuit of that elusive scent. You will keep the falcon on your fist or on the cadge, preferably with its hood on. Eventually the dog's sensitive nose will catch the tantalizing smell of game and it will come to a halt. A reliable worker will hold its point for a considerable time, giving you the chance to unhood the falcon and launch it into the air. It will quickly learn the routine and, climbing into the wind (and, co-incidentally, over the as yet unseen quarry) will mount up over the dog, waiting for the flush. The presence of the falcon will make the game sit tighter, so there is little chance of an unplanned flush happening.

With a young or inexperienced falcon you will want to make a wide circle around the area to get upwind of the game. The falcon's training should lead it to expect you to produce the lure once it begins waiting on above you. This will mean that it is now circling over you, but more importantly, upwind of the game. When you feel that it is well enough positioned, at a height that will give it a good chance, you should yell the same command you use for giving it the lure. This command should be exactly the same one you have taught the dog to respond to when you want it to flush game. At the same time as the dog springs forward you should run in towards it.

The quarry is between a rock and a hard place. With you and the falcon coming from one direction and the pointer from the other, it will opt to fly over the pointer. This will be downwind, that is, in the same direction as the wind is blowing. The wind strength will be greater up high than it will be close to the ground. Because of this your falcon, benefiting from the advantage of added height, will be travelling much faster than its quarry. The latter, being swept along by the wind, cannot gain height or change direction. This makes it

an easier target for the falcon to hit. Of course the falcon may fail to catch anything at first, but it will quickly learn the sequence of events and, in anticipating them, will become more adept.

With accipiters and buteos people use a variety of different dogs. I have hunted over terriers, whippets, collies, labradors, springers, and the full range of pointing and HPR (hunt, point, retrieve) breeds. Anything that will push game out is of use, but, with most breeds the dog will simply flush it at random, away from you and the bird. Since game birds are able to fly much faster than most hawks, you are likely to have little success, and will spend a lot of time going to recover your hawk following unsuccessful flights. An energetic dog, rummaging through thick cover or working hedge bottoms, will probably cost you as many flights as it will provide. Instead it makes sense to buy a pointing or HPR breed. These, when they find game, will go on point. You are now in charge of the situation and can 'stage manage' it to get the best chase.

Knowing where your game is will enable you to choose the direction in which you will flush it. By approaching from the side offering the greatest amount of cover, you can force the quarry to escape towards more open terrain. You may be able to cast your hawk into a nearby tree and drive the pheasant or rabbit in that direction. Perhaps you want simply to make it run downhill, to give your bird a more inviting chase. At any rate you are now in control. The hawk can rely on your efficiency to find quarry for it, and to present it with a good chase.

It may not suit you to have a dog. They require time and attention that you may find difficult to provide on a daily basis. A less demanding alternative, but still an essential one for the rabbiting hawker, are a couple of ferrets. You will soon learn to spot evidence of rabbit populations, and their warrens are visible for the world to see. The ferret will drive out the inhabitants and afford your bird the chance of a chase. It is easier to catch

Dogs can mark the best hole to ferret and will save you wasting time on unoccupied warrens.

rabbits this way than to rely on flushing them from cover. The ferreted rabbit is running from a sanctuary and has to cross open ground to reach the next hole, while the rabbit flushed from cover will head towards the nearest warren and is already halfway there.

In some areas there are an awful lot of warrens. For every one that holds rabbits there may be a dozen that are empty. Working these can be boring, unproductive and tiring for the ferret. Your dog, with very little encouragement, will learn to mark occupied warrens, even indicating the hole that has the nearest resident. This makes ferreting much more fun and certainly makes for good ferrets and good hawks.

Entering Your Hawk or Falcon to Game

It is illegal in the UK to use bagged game (that is live quarry which is released in an enclosed space or in an area it does not know). I have never needed to do this with any bird, and usually get a kill on the bird's first hunting day. Currently I am flying three Harris hawks which all killed the first time they were flown loose. Neither do I use dummy bunnies as lures. All I do is feed them off the entire carcasses of their intended quarry before they are picked up for training. This applies also to falcons. They all recognize the live version!

Obtaining Dead Game

Even having to ask about this makes me question what chance of success your bird will have. But it is a question I have heard many times.

Many novice falconers fail to practise finding and flushing game before they get a bird. Why ever not? You will learn where game lies, which way it will go and how close

114

you can get to it. It certainly makes the real thing a lot easier.

If you are going to use a ferret you might as well blow the family budget on a handful of purse nets as well. That way you will have a supply of rabbits to feed your un-entered bird on, and to drag about as lures if necessary. Other game may be shot (with an air rifle, not a shotgun – unless you like picking pellets out of the corpse). Avoid road kills unless they are large enough to remove the head and organs. There is always the risk of these carrying poisons or pesticides. If you are intending hunting crow, rook or magpie your local shoot will be more than happy to supply the contents of its Larsen traps.

It is no good saying you do not know how to ferret, or where a gamekeeper may be located. You are the one who wants to hunt, you have got permission on hunting land and you have practised before you got your bird – haven't you?

GETTING YOUR BIRD OFF ITS QUARRY

When your hawk or falcon is on its quarry there is a possibility that the victim may still be alive. Always make haste to dispatch it as quickly and humanely as possible.

Killing Game
Even if you are familiar with doing this your bird will make it more complicated. Almost certainly it will have its victim by the head. It will be hanging on grimly and its feet will not be shifting about. Even so you dare not use a knife in case your bird moves its grip and you sever the hawk's toes. A priest (the weighted stick used by fisherman to kill fish) is no better: while you may not cut your bird's toes off you may still break them. Some falconers, particularly ladies who lack physical strength, use a sharp spike set in a handle, like a gimlet. Most of us simply use our hands to wring the neck of birds or break the neck of rabbits and hares. With small quarry you may not be able

to get a sufficiently good grip to enable you to break its neck. Particularly with rats, squirrels, stoats and snakes, all of which can bite the bird, I do not stand on ceremony but just crush the head with the end of my stick. Whatever method you use, you must be efficient and quick.

Practice will improve you. As an exercise, obtain the carcasses of game and try to put a knife or gimlet through the heart and other vital organs. Then skin the carcass and see how close you got. You should not experiment with live game in the field.

Your hawk meanwhile will not appreciate your interference, which is another reason for dispatching your quarry swiftly. Once the creature is dead you can let your novice bird pull at its victim a bit. Being allowed to do this with you nearby is no different in its mind to feeding at home with you beside its perch.

Removing a Kill from Your Bird
Once your hawk has been allowed as much or as little time on its kill as you think fit (see below), you can 'make in' to remove the quarry. If your bird is showing signs of jealousy, by mantling and trying to drag its kill away, you must take your time. Being patient now will save you so much stress in the future.

Stand back a little until your bird starts pulling at the carcass. Every time its head goes down, it is telling you that it feels comfortable with your proximity. This is when you slowly edge in, probably on your knees in the mud. The slightest move on your part may make it stop feeding and look up, which it would normally do between each mouthful anyway. When it does this you must stay still, edging in again as its head returns to the kill.

Eventually, if you have been patient enough, you will have your glove or hawking bag over your hawk's feet, hiding the kill from its sight. For simplicity I would always advise that at this stage you throw a meaningful titbit far enough to one side that your bird cannot reach it without releasing its grip, but close enough for the tempting morsel to be clearly seen. A chick's head is a suitably sized bribe. Given a choice between holding on to something that has disappeared (its kill) and going for a visible reward, your bird will always plump for the latter. Some birds anticipate this procedure to the extent that they will step off a kill without you having to cover it first.

You have now got the game hidden under the hawking bag and the hawk swallowing a small reward. Offer another piece of food on your glove. Hey presto, the bird is safely back on your fist and its jesses can be secured around your fingers. Only then do you attempt to get the game into the bag. At this moment you may discover that you have failed to kill the game. More than one falconer has suffered the embarrassment of seeing their quarry beating an unexpected and hasty retreat. This is really unforgivable. The escaping animal or bird will be getting away on adrenalin; once it has gone to ground or got to cover, it may suffer a long death from septicaemia (an infection of its wounds) or internal bleeding.

A warren that I hunted had a single black individual among its rabbit population. This was chased one day and hit by two of my female Harris hawks. To its credit it made good its escape. Some weeks later it was not so lucky and it ended up in my game bag. When I skinned it I found that the whole of one back leg, and most of the saddle of its back, was covered in a huge abscess. I am certain that this was the result of its previous near miss, and it must have been in terrible agony for all of that intervening time.

Feeding the Bird on a Kill

When I got my first proper hunting bird I resolved to let it feed up on its kills, albeit on my glove, for the whole of its first season. This was frustrating if it killed within the first few minutes of what was intended to be a prolonged session, but I still felt that this was an investment in its future good behaviour. It was always good to pick up. The success of

---

What Can Go Wrong?

- If you 'make in' too quickly your hawk may carry the game off.
- If you fail to dispatch the victim properly before bribing the hawk off it, you may well have the frustrating and embarrassing spectacle of it disappearing. I cannot think of a falconer this has not happened to!
- If the bird sees you pulling bits of food out of your bag you may end up with it sticking its talons into you in an effort to get to the bribe as quickly as possible.
- Failure to throw the bribe far enough will result in the hawk swallowing it while still hanging on to its kill.
- Not securing your hawk on the fist before you try to put the game in the bag could see you ending up in an undignified tug-of-war with it, at best. At worst you could very easily find the hawk attached to your hand. Don't worry. Having a ventilated hand is one of the 'rights of passage' for a falconer.

---

this training convinced me that this was the way to do it.

Subsequently I was reluctantly forced, by circumstance, to bribe a young bird off her kills from the very first day. That bird, too, was always excellent to take from a carcass. Now I have come to expect multiple kills in a day, even from novice birds, and have no problems, either with their keenness or with bribing them off.

What seems to be the deciding factor is the extent to which an individual hawk is 'sticky-footed'. Some lock on for ages, no matter how patient you are. With one bird of mine, a prolific and experienced hunter, I have given up trying to bribe her off kills and just rip them away from her. It looks as if she is badly mannered but in fact she is simply unable to let go. In my experience, while most sticky-footed birds are good hunters, a lot of good hunters are not sticky-footed.

Although it is good to feed a bird from its first few kills and the occasional one thereafter, it is not as vital as you might think.

NATURAL HAWKING HAZARDS

Visibility Problems

Snow, low cloud and fog make it impossible to see your bird. If the problem is likely to be temporary, you can expect your bird to be fairly near at hand, but hunting is difficult if not foolhardy.

Wet Weather

Heavy rain will soak your bird, and it may roost in a tree and refuse to come to you. This makes sense to it. Why on earth should it fly when there is nothing to chase and every flap of its wings renders it more and more waterlogged?

Sometimes showery weather can hamper you. A sudden squall of rain can dampen your hawk's wings and make it unwilling or unable to fly. Then the sun comes out and eventually it becomes dry enough for you to try again. Naturally this is the cue for the rain to come down again. Such a sequence can go on for hours, and is immensely frustrating.

One solution is to carry a plastic carrier bag in your pocket. This should be trimmed so that it is as long as the bird's body. Then cut a round hole in the bottom. Invert this and pop it over the hawk's head, and you have a portable raincoat for it. Birds will quickly become used to it, and once they do, you simply cover them while it is raining and then take it off as the sun comes out, and you have a dry bird.

Hot Weather

Mostly birds cope well with very hot conditions, although a sudden change in temperature can lead to them being a bit lazy until they adjust. The principal danger is that they may choose to go up on a thermal. Falcons in particular seem to get drunk on thermals, and lose all track of time. Perhaps they are content to lie there, weightless, watching the world revolve underneath them. At any rate they can stay on a good thermal for hours and drift slowly with it. After some

Harris hawk in a portable 'rain mac'. They quickly get used to wearing these.

time they decide that they are hungry, or the thermal simply cools down and they descend to look for food. Unfortunately they have no idea where you or they are. I have had falcons travel over a 150km (93miles) in this way in a matter of hours.

I once watched a very experienced Harris hawk slowly circling upwards on a thermal. The tiny dot gradually vanished into a cloudless blue sky. By some strange working of fate it eventually landed, several kilometres away, on the garden fence of a falconer, but I would not expect to be so lucky again.

Cold

This should never be an issue when flying a healthy bird of prey. Their feathers provide superb insulation. I have flown a Harris hawk in 20° below freezing point without any hint of a problem. However, the perched Harris,

The result of wingtip oedema caused by frostbite. This Harris hawk is still an excellent hunter but has difficulty flying uphill.

especially if it has got wet, may get frostbite in its wings and develop wingtip oedema, which in extreme cases can result in them losing the last part of their wing.

I had a female Harris that suffered from this condition. For a couple of days she had exhibited a reluctance to fly, and I could see that her wings were uncomfortable. I was carrying her across the yard when she flapped her wings. To my horror both wingtips snapped off. The last four or five feathers and the tissue from which they grew simply fell on the ground and lay there like a pair of hands.

Never having experienced this condition before I did not know the extent to which it would disable her. The next day I tried to get her to come a short distance to me. She reluctantly scrambled and flapped, crabwise, on to my fist. It looked terrible. At that moment I felt that she would never fly again. Certainly hunting would be beyond her. Breeding was not an option, as her mother had suffered from the same condition, and I suspected that the daughter carried a hereditary predisposition towards it. I reluctantly contemplated euthanasia.

Having slept on the problem, I rose in the morning with no fresh inspiration to lift my mood. However, the hawk seemed a little less sore, so I decided to try to exercise her around a small paddock where she could walk along the stone walls if she did not want to fly. By the time we had completed the circuit she had killed three rabbits! Needless to say she returned to the hunting team, where she continues to this day. She cannot fly uphill for any distance, but downhill or on the level she is still successful. She has had to develop a faster wing beat to remain airborne, and is quite quick off the mark.

If there is any likelihood of frost you should ensure that your Harris is kept indoors at least 1.2m (4ft) above ground. Of course, no wet bird of prey should be put in the mews until it is completely dry.

Working in a Wind

High winds will possibly blow a bird of prey away. However, I flew all my birds in the famous 'hurricane' of 1987 and did not lose a single one. A fit bird can work in a gale, but may be unwilling to battle back to you if it

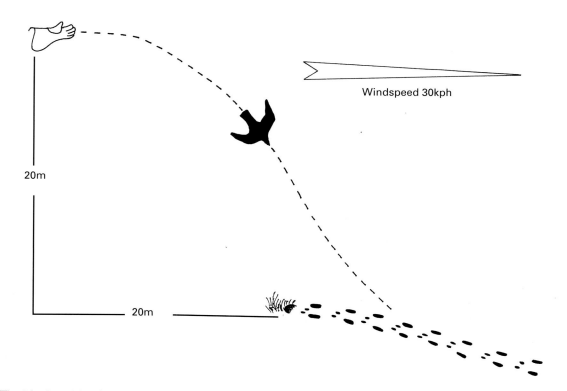

Windspeed 30kph

20m

20m

The ideal position for a downwind slip on level ground.

does get swept away. It may have to stop several times, and can be seen to tack back and forth so that it is not flying directly into the wind.

Hunting ground game in windy conditions can test both your fieldcraft and your strategy. There is a difference between ground speed and air speed that you need to understand. The hawk is working in an environment that is moving continually in one direction. If the wind is travelling at 30kph, and the hawk is flying in the same direction at 50kph, it will pass stationary objects at a combined speed of 80kph. Going in the opposite way it will pass them at 20kph, as the air it is flying in will be carrying it backwards nearly as fast as it can travel forward. By contrast the rabbit (moving at about 30kph) can kick against

solid ground, and apart from a little wind resistance, can move just as fast whichever way it chooses to go.

This means that the hawk will struggle to overtake the rabbit when the latter runs into the wind. With the wind behind it, however, the hawk can rapidly catch up with the fastest rabbit. Unfortunately, the rabbit can turn and stop whereas the hawk cannot – and even if it could it would still be swept past by the wind. This means that slipping it with the wind behind it will be equally unsuccessful. The only way to achieve a reasonable chance is to position the bird a good distance upwind, but well out to the side. This will force the quarry to run downwind, so it does not matter how much start you give it. The hawk can easily pull this back but it needs time to build up

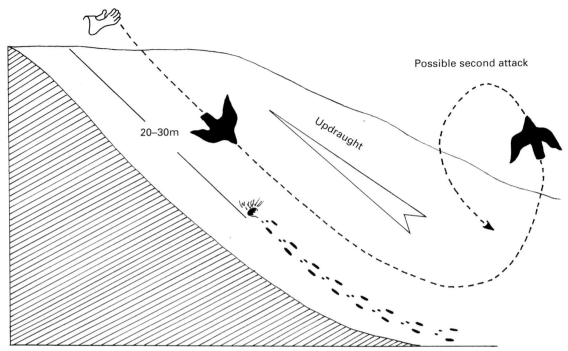

The easiest slip is downhill and into the wind. The slope gives the bird speed and the wind gives it control and manoeuvrability.

enough speed to cut across the wind. This gives it the opportunity to do so and thus be able to turn with the rabbit. The odds are still in the rabbit's favour, but you have maximized your bird's chances.

Hill Winds

These can help or hinder you. The best situation is when the wind is coming straight at the sloping ground, which will give your bird lift. As always you need to be above your intended target so that your hawk has the advantage of height. The rabbit will have to run downhill, away from you, and this puts it at a severe disadvantage. With its short front legs and long hind ones it will be over-striding. It is committed to running straight down the hill, and cannot easily turn or stop unless it finds some flat ground. For the bird the chase is easy, just a question of gliding down, hugging the contours of the hill to avoid wind resistance. With the wind in its face the bird can twist and turn very easily. Even if the rabbit turns and runs uphill, the bird needs only to hit the wind to soar up and catch the rabbit as it climbs.

When the wind is coming from behind you things are very different. As it pours over the hill it will suck all the lift away from the hawk. You will still try to organize a downhill slip but this time the odds are very much in favour of the quarry. The hawk is being carried forward and is deprived of lift, brakes and steering. Stand well out to the side and above the game to have any chance of success. Expect a lot of rabbits to escape.

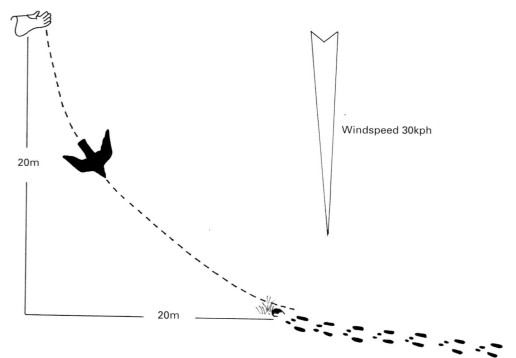

20m

20m

Windspeed 30kph

Slips in a side wind require you to stand a long way upwind.

Side Winds

Side winds also pose problems. Here again you need to be higher than the quarry but, if you are directly above it, the wind will sweep your bird past the line of the rabbit's vertical descent. You will need to stand well away to the windward so that the bird gains control of its flight at about the time it is above the rabbit.

Water

Hawks do plunge into ponds, particularly after moorhen. They can get dirty water into their lungs and die very quickly. Retrieving hawks and falcons from opposite banks or islands is not fun, and could be dangerous where currents or tides are strong. It is a good idea to know where bridges and fording places are in advance, or where boats are kept!

Retrieving hawks from the opposite bank is not fun, so avoid hawking by rivers or near lakes that have islands in them.

Power lines are usually far enough apart not to affect a single bird but these Harris hawks could easily bridge across the wires if they extended their wings at the same time.

Resident Birds and Animals

Other birds of prey may drive your hawk out of their territory, and rooks, crows and gulls can also be very aggressive. A tame hawk is at risk from fox or dogs if it is on the ground with a kill. I have even had a falcon trampled to death by inquisitive cattle in this way. The danger presented by some quarry species is covered in the next chapter.

MAN-MADE HAZARDS

Vehicular, Rail and Air Traffic

This is self-explanatory and will have a bearing on where you choose to fly your bird of prey. Major roads, railways, canals and rivers can all create tremendous logistical problems if your hawk or falcon kills on the opposite side. Apart from the sheer inconvenience of retrieving them, there is a very real risk of the bird being killed. I have heard of hawks landing in the middle of dual carriageways with fatal results, and one friend of mine, hawking in a railway cutting, had such a near miss with an Intercity express that his hawk came back with a talon ripped out.

Remember that it is not just the safety of your hawk that is at stake. It would be terrible to cause an accident in which a person was injured.

Electrical Power Lines and Transformers

Such things as electricity sub-stations can act as a magnet to your bird, with potentially fatal results. The very large power lines carry a static charge that will blow your bird off them. The cables are too far apart for the wings to bridge across them, but your hawk may land on a single cable. There will be a blue flash but the bird will survive unhurt.

Local power lines are only 137cm (54in) apart and can be bridged if two birds land on the pole together (Harris flyers beware). Also the cross bar, on which the lines are strung, is made of metal. I have had birds get a nasty shock on these in very wet weather, and think I was lucky not to lose one.

By most rural buildings there will be a small, pole-mounted transformer. The drop wires down to it from the power line are only 45cm (18in) apart, and this is where most fatalities occur. If you regularly fly in the same

Transformer boxes are lethal as the drop wires are so close that any bird can short-circuit across them.

place it is worth getting them insulated by the electric company. The cost is much less than replacing a hawk.

Falcons sometimes injure themselves by hitting high-tension cables while stooping on game – which use these for cover.

Glass-Fronted Buildings

Birds of all sorts fly into windows, and the bird of prey is no exception. They will sometimes crash into windows in pursuit of quarry which is hoping to make an escape through the room behind them. At other times birds of prey seem to attack their own reflection. It is fairly unusual for a hawk or falcon to kill themselves outright in this way, but they can be concussed or damage an eye.

Chimneys

I have had two odd experiences with chimneys and, although I have never heard of anyone else having similar problems, I doubt if I am unique. Firstly, I had an old lanner falcon go missing one day. She was a very experienced, reliable bird, and I could never work out why she should have vanished. Some years later a local builder who was

Razor wire is increasingly used and is highly dangerous to a hawk's feet.

123

working on a house in the village, presented me with a skeleton on which were jesses, bells and a ring. She had fallen down a chimney, possibly poisoned by carbon monoxide.

The second accident happened on a landfill site. Many of these contain bio-degradable waste, which slowly rots and produces significant amounts of methane. To eliminate the risk of this exploding, the operators install pipe systems to siphon off the gas. It is channelled into vents that are continually burning in a controlled way. The difficulty is that the flame is invisible. One bird chose to land on this isolated perch, which was virtually white hot. It suffered serious burns to both feet, as well as some pretty singed feathers. Amazingly it flew straight back on to the vent, and got burned a second time, before we could get to it.

Wire Fences

Like power lines, there is much anecdotal evidence of falcons amputating wings as they stoop through sheep and deer fences. Given the range of grouse and partridge it may be impossible to avoid such hazards. With the current trend for ever-greater security your bird may also come across razor wire.

Shooting

You should have permission, but others may have too. Check with the farmer or land-owner whether this is the case. If there are other people using the land it is necessary to contact them, and make sure that they will not shoot your bird – either deliberately or by accident.

ETHICS

Public Relations

As a falconer you have a responsibility to represent the sport and to portray it in a good light. For most of the time the general public will not criticize you, but there is a vociferous minority who will take you to task. Quite

possibly you may be in a no-win situation, as the other person is coming from a pre-conceived and emotionally based position. No amount of coherent argument will prevail so just be polite and maintain your own dignity.

What you must never do is give just cause for complaint. In any walk of life it is always our own side that fails us most miserably. Ensure that your behaviour, and that of your hawk, is beyond reproach.

Even if it is inconvenient be prepared to stop your hawking to talk to ramblers. Show an awareness of other people's feelings by not boasting about your kills, speak instead of the pleasure you get from watching the bird exercise its natural skills – and the admiration you have for the ones that get away. Be generous with your time in educating children and their parents. Agree to go to schools, cub packs, and so on if you feel able to do so. If not, give them the address of a falconry centre or club that can help.

An awareness of the environment and conservation should be second nature to a falconer. Use this knowledge to emphasize the prey/predator balance, and the raptor's role as nature's quality controller. Stress that falconry is natural one-on-one hunting, with no injured quarry left at the end of the day, and emphasize the high mortality rate of the bird of prey in the wild. Explain the importance of birds of prey as apex predators (at the top of the food chain). They can only survive if everything else is doing well and so their success is an important way of monitoring the health of the environment.

Insurance

Third party and public liability insurance is essential. You may automatically have cover if you are a member of the Countryside Alliance or any other body which represent field sports. If you do not have this membership then you really should get it immediately. Apart from the security this insurance offers, these organizations are the ones that represent your sport in the political arena, both in the UK and in Europe. They will provide legal advice and can help in dealing with the media. It is important that they are properly funded to do this.

Legal Responsibilities

- Your bird must be legally in captivity (*see* Chapter 5).
- You must have the landowner's permission (preferably in writing), and a current Game Licence, acquired from the post office for the princely sum (currently) of £6 for a calendar year.
- If you intend making any sort of charge for flying your bird to the public you must have a Performing Animals Licence from your county council. Most county councils are unaware of this and make up their own fees as they go along. Since the Article 10 Certificate licenses the commercial use of European birds of prey the Performing Animals Licence is largely redundant except for birds from other continents.
- You must be aware that there are laws to protect the welfare of animals and birds. This applies not only to your bird, but also to the quarry you will chase. At all times you must strive be humane and caring.

Quarry

Observe the game seasons, which are designed to protect quarry from over-hunting, and during the breeding season.

When hawking ensure that all quarry is dispatched humanely and promptly, and respect the individual quarry that has bested you. It will be there another day, hopefully having reproduced its own likeness.

Avoid taking domestic poultry or small pets. Nobody made you go so close to where they might be. If an accident does happen you must tell the owners and make what amends you can.

CHAPTER 8

The Quarry

In the British Isles falconers and austringers are blessed with a wide variety of wildlife that they can pursue with their birds. All ground and flying game falls within three categories: protected species, game species and vermin. To some extent even the last group is protected, as it is illegal to cause them unnecessary suffering or to kill them in ways that are not sanctioned by law.

PROTECTED SPECIES

This covers the vast majority of creatures and birds within our countryside. Deliberately hunting them is illegal without a specific Quarry Licence, which is obtainable by application to the relevant authority (*see* box). Licences to intentionally take trad-itional quarry species, such as blackbirds (with sparrowhawks) and skylarks (the proper quarry of merlins), will normally be issued but may restrict the number and even locality where this is permitted. The list of protected species is reviewed regularly to include any that have become rarer, or to exclude those that may have reached pest status.

GAME SPECIES

This category includes all species of game birds, wildfowl that are not on the protected list, and deer and hare. There are specified seasons for hunting these which vary according to species and locality. A Game Licence can be obtained from your local main

---

Issuing Authorities for Quarry Licences

England:
DEFRA, Wildlife Licensing & Registration Service
Zone 1/17
Temple Quay House
2 The Square
Temple Quay
Bristol BS1 6EB
Tel: 0117 372 6098
www.defra.gov.uk

Scotland:
The Environment & Rural Affairs Department (ERAD)
Pentlands House
47 Robbs Loan
Edinburgh EH14 1TY
Tel: 0131 244 6231

Wales:
National Assembly for Wales
Agriculture Department
Yr Hen Ysgol Gymrag
Ffordd Alexandra
Aberystwyth
Ceredigion SY23 1LD
Tel: 01970 627762

Northern Ireland:
John Milburne
Environment & Heritage Service
35 Castle Street
Belfast BT1 1GU
Tel: 02890 546558

---

post office for the princely sum of £6. This permits you to hunt all game species for a twelve-month period.

VERMIN

Some species of mammals and birds are scheduled as being vermin, including rabbits, squirrels, rats, mice, feral pigeons, magpies, crows, stoats and weasels. They are perceived to be pests within the countryside, and as such have little protection. This may be because they destroy crops and woodland, are a threat to livestock, game and wildlife, or represent a health hazard. Invariably pest species are numerous, and it is easy to get permission from landowners to hunt them. This list of species is regularly reviewed to reflect the changing population levels – for example starlings and house sparrows have now been removed from this list.

MAMMALS

Deer
We have six species of deer in Britain: the red, roe, fallow, sikha, muntjac and Chinese water deer. Of these only the first two are native, although the fallow has been with us since Roman times and is an established resident. Over recent years there has been a boom in deer numbers, to the extent that they are now doing appreciable damage to forestry plantations and crops, and are even invading suburban gardens. This means that the falconer may stumble across them quite often. Any bird that will tackle such large quarry with any hope of success is not suitable for use in most parts of Britain. Hunting them with birds of prey should be confined to eagles, and kept to remote areas. You will need a game licence.

Foxes
Like deer, foxes are widespread and may be encountered often. The same reservations exist with regard to their suitability as quarry as for deer. Apart from eagles it would be possible to catch one with a large, female red-tailed hawk. However, the risk to the bird,

and the fact that the carcass has no food value, means that there is little point in contemplating this as bona fide prey.

Brown Hares
This is one of the classic game species. Over recent years their numbers have fluctuated because of disease, so be conscious of the need to treat them as a conservation case in those areas where they have become scarce. I have frequently found that farmers and landowners have a special fondness for hares, so check that you will not be causing offence to your host by chasing them.

Brown hares live exclusively above ground. To catch one is always a test of your bird's speed, stamina and courage. Not all birds will relish a struggle with such a powerful opponent, and some go off the idea after a few kickings. Respect their judgement, as they are the ones being beaten up.

Brown hares may suddenly jump up from under your feet as you walk across the fields. A close slip like this is ideal with a novice bird. It will take off as a reflex action and may catch the hare without having had time to think twice. Your job will be to get to them as soon as possible. The less your bird has to struggle with its victim on its own, the more confident it will be on future occasions. Because of the hare's liking for open fields you may be able to mark one down from a distance and stalk up to it. This is more difficult than it sounds, as a hare can hide in the slightest bit of cover. A line of beaters is probably the best technique for flushing hares.

A good dog will point a hare. This enables you to choose which way to flush it to give your bird the best chance. Unfortunately a lot of dogs are not able to resist chasing the hare as well. By pursuing the hare they encourage it to run faster than it might otherwise do, making it harder for your hawk to catch it. The sight of a hare, followed in succession by a rioting dog, a hawk and an enraged falconer, has entertained many a falconry field meeting.

Blue Hares

Blue hares are smaller and slighter than their brown cousins. They are protected by their choice of mountain habitat as they are rarely found below 600m (2,000ft). From this vantage point they can see you toiling up the hill towards them and encourage you onwards by moving just a little bit ahead of you, and then sitting up to make sure you are following. As long as they are on a slope you have little chance of success. The hawk cannot possibly fly fast enough uphill to overtake them. On level ground, or better still if you can get above them, you are in control. Your hawk can chase them confidently. Until the last moment that is, when they jink to one side and then canter comfortably up to the next level.

Sometimes a blue hare will disappear from sight in a seemingly open expanse of land. Close inspection of the area where you last saw it may reveal a hole under some rocks, or even in the side of a peat hag. I always take a ferret with me on blue hare hunts for this eventuality. The hare has gone to ground but its burrow is only a metre or two long. The ferret will have it out pretty quickly, and if hearing a rabbit rumbling around underground is exciting, this sounds like someone beating a bass drum down there.

In my experience a dog is of little value when blue hare hawking, as the hares are normally very visible anyway. The presence of a dog only encourages them to move up higher than ever. The best way to hunt them is to stalk the hill they are on. Plan your campaign before you start and do not get sidetracked from it. Determine which hill you are going to hunt and then climb its neighbour to get round and above the hares. You will only catch them with the advantage of height.

The blue hare is less robust than its brown cousin and is more easily held, but is still a very worthwhile adversary. This challenge, and the remoteness and beauty of their habitat, makes blue hare hawking one of the classic chases.

Cats

Cats are never deliberately hunted but do crop up where not expected. Most hawks can deal with one, but they are dangerous and to be avoided wherever possible. I have taken Scottish wildcat and found them no more difficult than feral or domestic cats. If you do have to disentangle your hawk from one you will be grateful for your falconry gauntlet. Apart from their teeth, cats also have formidable claws on both front and back feet.

Rabbits

Thank God for the rabbit! The humble bunny is plentiful and within the scope of most large hawks and buteos. It is very rare for a bird to be injured by one. Although they will try to buck a hawk off they do not bite. One possible danger is that they can sometimes drag a hawk down their burrow. Once there it cannot back out easily and may stay underground until it dies. I lost a male Harris in this way, and it took me weeks to work out what had happened. Now I would be better prepared and would listen very closely for the sound of a bell at all the possible holes. Failing this, I would explore every tunnel by hand or with a stick to try to find the hawk.

In good weather, rabbits will feed quite a distance from their warren, and may take shelter in rough grass, bracken, nettles or reeds. It is always worth beating such clumps of vegetation with your stick. You never know. I have found them (or more correctly my dogs have found them) hidden in rolls of fencing, inside old pipes and rollers and quite high in hollow trees.

All rabbits are fitted with overdrive and 'all-wheel steering'. They can stop dead, jump back over an incoming bird, climb sheer rock faces and occasionally even take to water. They know every hole and where there is a gap in every fence. In short they are very worthy opponents. Mostly, however, the rabbit will be tucked away in its nice, snug bury. Your dog may have pointed this or you may have seen the rabbit run for home. In all cases be quiet and stealthy. Work out where the next nearest warren is and try to cut off that line of retreat. When you have decided where best to place your hawk it is time to slip the ferret in. With luck you will get a good chase and a successful conclusion.

Sometimes a rabbit will sit in the mouth of a warren before bolting. It is weighing up the dangers and, if you are over-eager and slip your hawk too soon, you may see it pop back down the hole again. You now have a real problem because the rabbit knows exactly what is waiting for it and will not want to come out. The fact that there is a ferret with it will not be as frightening as you might expect. In its rabbit mind it will be happier facing danger in the security of its hole than above ground. Be prepared for a long wait and the unrewarding sight of the ferret emerging with a bloody muzzle where it has killed underground.

For this same reason you should resist the temptation to ferret a hole into which your hawk has chased a rabbit. There may be other rabbits in there but they have been alerted to the danger by the thumping feet of the escapee. Even if they bolt quickly your ferret will not rest until the very last one is out or killed, and this is invariably the one you chased down in the first place. It has probably gone to the deepest part of the warren and is blocking the tunnel by hunching its back and imitating a fur-covered boulder. Your ferret will scratch and scrabble away at its backside, but will simply fill its own claws with fur until they resemble furry carpet slippers. With these it will make little impression on the rabbit, and you may have to wait a very long time to get your ferret back.

Grey Squirrels

Note that red squirrels are protected.

These tree rats offer some of the most exciting chases. They are much too dangerous for the hawk, however, and should be avoided. Grey squirrels give a really severe bite, and many hawks have lost the use of toes as a result. Experienced birds learn to go for

Tree-climbing skills may be called for if your hawk starts squirrel hunting in earnest.

the head, not the tail. Red-tailed hawks seem able to tolerate the bites more easily. In the US, falconers go group-hawking for squirrels with passage red-tails (which have learnt in the wild not to attack each other). They protect their birds' feet by fitting special anklets and extended toe covers, that are covered with bright brass studs. The squirrel tends to bite at these.

Any hawks that have done a lot of squirrel hawking get very committed to this quarry. Such a bird cannot be allowed to self-hunt from trees, as they will be constantly scanning for squirrel activity. They sometimes learn to attack squirrel dreys (nests), ripping them apart in an effort to flush out potential residents. The worst-case scenario, which happens far too frequently, is that your bird catches a squirrel up a tree and stays there. This is most undesirable as the bird's feet can be severely bitten. If you cannot reach it the hawk will eventually gorge itself – and be totally indifferent to your bribes and entreaties. There are few experiences as depressing, at the end of a day, as having to leave a hawk up a tree. Faced with this unwelcome situation you may discover tree-climbing skills you never knew you had.

Squirrels are spotted visually, although my dogs can get very excited by squirrel hawking, and will point trees containing them. You sometimes find that a hunted one, driven out of the trees by the hawks, will take refuge in a rabbit hole. My own advice is to leave them there, but if your blood is up and your hawk's blood is up, you may be foolish enough to try to get it out. This is easy as they will not face a ferret and come out very promptly.

Should your hawk catch a squirrel, whether by accident or design, your first responsibility is to immobilize the squirrel's head and teeth. Dispatch squirrels with a knife or a spike, or quickly crush their skulls with your stick. Then check your bird's feet for bites. When I have to use my antiseptic spray on a bird, 90 per cent of the time it is for squirrel bites.

Stoats, Weasels, Mink, Polecats and Ferrets

These all fall prey to hawks at some time or another. Apart from biting badly they also have musk glands that they release when scared. I won't spoil your fun – you will find out for yourself. One hawk of mine, after killing two stoats in one ten-minute period, still stunk of them five months later and was definitely a bird to hold at arm's length! Because of their small size I find it tricky to

kill them with a knife. It is, however, fairly easy just to crush the skull with your stick – not nice but necessary.

Rats

Like grey squirrels, rats offer fast and exciting sport. They also bite dangerously and carry Weil's disease, which is fatal to people. I suggest you avoid rats. If your bird does catch one you must never handle it with bare hands.

Mice, Voles and Other Small Rodents

These are a nuisance, as hawks will catch them with relish – and swallow them in one. All you get is a fat hawk and nothing in the game bag. They cannot be avoided.

BIRDS

Unlike mammals, birds are unlikely to injure your hawk.

Grouse and Partridge

If you have access to land that holds these you are lucky. Grouse and partridge are principally suited to being hunted with falcons that can stoop off a height, but the true accipiters can reasonably take partridge in level flight. The buteos are too slow through the air to be likely to overhaul any of these, although partridge sometimes get taken in a hedge bottom or thick cover. They offer good eating for you and your hawk or falcon, and no danger of your bird being injured. Dispatch them humanely by pulling their necks.

Grouse and partridge live in family groups or coveys. At the start of the season these may number up to twenty individuals, but predation whittles them down to single figures as the season wears on. Coveys may be spotted visually but they have the knack of filtering away through the ground cover. You may find that the area you had confidently marked them down in is now curiously empty, so you will need a pointing dog.

A hen pheasant in cover can be almost invisible without a dog to help you detect it.

Pheasant

The shooting fraternity releases so many pheasants each year that plenty wander off the shooting estates and on to other land. In most parts of the country the optimistic falconer can reasonably hope to come across one or two of these strays. They tend to be pretty visible on open fields and are easily seen from a distance. In wooded areas, or indeed in the lightest cover, they have the ability to disappear completely. The hens are camouflaged naturally, but the gaudy cocks can be equally hard to spot. If they think they are hidden they can be nearly impossible to flush. On one occasion, admittedly in quite

tussocky grass, I could not understand why my dog was pointing my boots. Closer inspection revealed that a cock pheasant was crouched under some loose grass between my feet!

Goshawks, and the occasional brave sparrowhawk, can take pheasant in a tail-chase. The buteos need the advantage of height to catch them on the rise. Positioning your hawk in a tree is excellent if you can flush the bird that way. I once had my dog on point in an overgrown ditch with my Harris in a dead tree above. The dog flushed ten pheasants out and the hawk ignored them all. The very last one, the eleventh, was the one it had been watching all along. To my disgust it

Use a hairdryer to dry out your hawk before putting it into the mews at night.

managed to miss that one as well!

When a pheasant is flushed the young hawk will follow it and, if you are lucky, will either get it as it re-enters cover or will mark where it has gone in, enabling you to re-flush the pheasant. The second flush is much more likely to be successful, as pheasants tend to burn all their energy up on the first escape. A hawk that has been thus rewarded will tend to persevere after pheasant in future, and will enjoy much success.

By and large I find pheasant hawking a bit uninteresting. You either get the bird on the ground or you watch it and your hawk disappearing into the distance. If you are fortunate you may eventually find it on a kill, which is great for the larder, but it is a poor spectacle.

Wildfowl

This category includes most ducks, geese, moorhens and coots. Several species of duck are now protected and must not be hawked, so make sure you are up to date with this. The only problem – and this applies to all wildfowl – is that they live near water, and tend to get themselves killed on the far side of rivers or on islands.

Sometimes your bird may actually bind to them in water and get a ducking for their trouble. At this point I panic. Although the hawk or falcon will usually be able to row to the bank, it will be wet through, and will soon get chilled. More importantly it may have ingested some water. A hawk belonging to a friend of mine died within twenty-four hours of doing this. The post mortem revealed that a small quantity of dirty pond water had got into its lungs. Nowadays I get my hawk to the veterinary surgeon immediately and get it put on a course of broad-spectrum antibiotics. Wet birds can be dried thoroughly with a hair-dryer, but be careful not to heat the rings or bells on its legs.

For falconers without a pointing dog, it should be possible to train your bird to wait on over dew ponds and the like, where you know ducks are present. You can then try to flush them under your bird, but be prepared for this to be a lot harder than you imagined. With a bird of prey above them they will prove adept at diving and hiding under bankside vegetation. You will have little idea of which direction they will take and you may have a long walk to find a successful falcon.

Snipe and Woodcock

These brilliant birds requiring merlins, perlins (peregrine × merlins), barbary tiercels or sparrowhawks if they are to be caught in flight. Goshawks and Harrises can and will take woodcock on the rise or in cover. Your bird will need to be flown from the fist as you cannot plan for the appearance of these wonderful flyers. Even a good pointing dog will rarely give reliable indication of snipe and woodcock. If you do get a flight at them be prepared to run a long way.

Waders

Waders are plentiful if you are working marshland and estuaries. Water remains a hazard for you. Do remember that tides can turn quickly, and run very fast, so channels may fill and you can get cut off. It is also possible to have a falcon go down in the sea and get swept away on an ebb tide. Hawks are unlikely to achieve much by way of results with waders.

Pigeons

These are plentiful but not ideal for high-flying falcons. You cannot present them from a point, and whenever the falcon mounts up it will see a pigeon and will rake off after it – a good way to lose falcons. Feral pigeons are also vectors of diseases that can transfer to birds of prey. Collar doves make superb sparrowhawk quarry and, as they carry salmonella, are justifiably killed near grain and sugar beet silos. The woodpigeon is sometimes taken on the nest by hawks flown in the summer months. A headlong dive into a thorn bush may result in an explosion of feathers as the pigeon meets its end. But what are you doing hunting quarry (even if it is vermin) during the breeding season?

Skylarks

This is a specialist quarry for the merlin men. You need a quarry licence for this and they are not readily given. Traditionally it was thought that merlins lost interest in, or the ability to catch, skylarks as the season progressed. Now it has been found that the young skylarks carry a lot of fat, which slows them down. As this gets burnt up they become faster than the merlin. With the onset of shorter daylight hours in winter, the skylark gets heavier and can once again be caught.

Blackbirds, Thrushes and Small Garden Birds

These are sparrowhawk fodder and brilliant sport. Again licences are needed from DEFRA.

REPTILES AND AMPHIBIANS

Sometimes hawks will kill snakes, lizards, frogs and toads. Remember adders are venomous; your bird could get killed although you will probably survive with just a few days of flu-like symptoms. They cannot bite through a falconry glove, and in my experience the hawk always gets them behind the head. Crush the head with your stick, which is not so easy as the hawk's feet seem to get everywhere.

Toads do not do much for the hawk's well-being either and seem pretty unpalatable. In Spring, toads and frogs are full of spawn, which gets all over the hawk's beak and feet – and sets like concrete!

CHAPTER 9

Associated Animals

The serious falconer or hawker will soon realize that he or she needs expert help when it comes to producing game for the hawk or falcon to chase. An army of beaters is all very well but is often so noisy that it is counter-productive. Wildlife hears them so far in advance that it has ample time to hide before your team gets there. There are other ways.

FERRETS

These convenient little creatures can be kept quite readily in hutches in the garden. They are very active at times, however, and benefit from an extended run or play area. It is best to keep more than one together. Either sex will work but the greater size of the males (hobs) makes them more likely to kill rabbits underground, and therefore less desirable, than their smaller sisters (jills). They also come in two basic colours – polecat, which is a dark brown background with lighter, fawn markings on the head and legs, and albino, which is white with pink eyes. Between these two are a host of subtle shades with a bewildering number of names.

Basically, it is best to use white ferrets for two reasons. Firstly it is easier to find them in undergrowth, and secondly the hawk should not confuse them with stoats, weasels, rabbits or other similar creatures in the heat of the moment.

Good ferrets are born and not made, but a good ferret can be made bad by thoughtless handling. They should be gentle when

Typically white jills are favoured by falconers. They are easily identified as not being quarry, are less able to kill rabbits underground than their bigger brothers and are less heavy to carry.

handled, come readily to the hand when working and should not lay up (that is, stay underground when they have killed a rabbit down there). A well-trained ferret should be tame and trusting enough to allow you to roll it into a ball, and throw it over the hedge for your partner to catch on the other side.

Getting a Good Ferret

The youngsters (kits) grow very slowly and it is illegal to sell a ferret that is under eight weeks old. At this age they are big enough to chew their own food and should be weaned. They might try to bite but their teeth lack strength, and a light tap on the nose with your finger should be sufficient to dissuade them. A young ferret that has been well-handled from this age should be a delight to work. It is not essential to buy a ferret at such a young age. Our own ferrets tend to get very little handling until they are picked up for work, at an age of four or five months. They enter readily to work, but if they show hesitancy at going into the warren it helps to work them with an older ferret initially.

Ferret rescue organizations get the ferrets that are useless, and ferrets are increasingly bred for the pet market. This does not mean that they may not be excellent workers, but it does reduce buying a ferret to a lottery and means that you are taking an unnecessary risk. Only buy from someone who works them. A clue to the possible temperament can be got from watching to see how easy the mother is to handle. If the seller is particularly careful you can guess she has a tendency to nip, and the chances are she will pass this on to her offspring.

Training the Hawk to Accept the Ferret

Both hawks and ferrets are professional killers. This means that there is always an element of risk in having the two around each other: I have lost a hawk to a ferret and vice versa. Your responsibility is to minimize the danger by creating familiarity. This will make the hawk tolerant of its little helper, although it will do little to stop the ferret attacking the bird.

The training consists of tethering the bird close to the ferret run. It will initially bate at

A hawk will wait in a tree above a warren and show no interest in the ferret as it wanders from hole to hole.

the ferret in an attempt to kill it. After a while it realizes that it is not succeeding and will give up. The sight of a ferret no longer triggers the prey reflex. Once the hawk accepts the sight of the ferret, both in its run and in your hands, the time has come to introduce them to the hawking field.

Always keep the hawk on your fist for your first ferreting expeditions. It will be distracted by everything else and will not bother with the familiar ferret. When it sees rabbits bolting from the warrens it will quickly associate the ferret with the production of rabbits. As long as it shows no reaction to the ferret and no obvious inclination to chase it, you may cast your hawk up into the branches above the warren. It will watch the ferret work and will be ideally placed for any rabbits that bolt.

Sometimes ferrets indulge in a mad five minutes when they emerge from the warren. They dance about, springing stiff-legged at your hand, and chattering to themselves. A bird that is really hungry may be tempted by all this activity. Anticipate trouble and get the bird back on the fist as quickly as possible.

When the hawk has missed a bolted rabbit that has re-entered the warren, it will be on the ground. If the ferret emerges at this point the hawk will almost certainly ignore it – its mind is on the rabbit. The inquisitive ferret, however, will wander up to the hawk to investigate. Get your hawk up and out of the way as quickly as possible or pick up the ferret. It would take only a second for the ferret to suddenly grab the hawk. One or the other of them is going to be badly hurt.

One of the reasons for using albino or white ferrets (you can get dark-eyed white individuals) is that the hawk can see immediately that it is not something to kill. This recognition is amazingly developed. Sometimes there will be a weasel or stoat already in the warren you are ferreting. These little chaps will not face even a small jill and will whizz out of the hole at a rate of knots. Hawks hate them and will crash in to catch them. Blessed with reflexes that work in nano-seconds, the stoat or weasel will double-back in its own length towards the sanctuary of the warren. With its blood up the hawk will be peering down the hole, only to be greeted by the sight of the ferret ambling out into the sunlight. Instead of footing it, as you might imagine, the hawk looks past it to where the stoat went. What never ceases to impress me is that they will do this even when the stoat is in its white winter coat.

Rabbit warrens contain unexpected things, and one of the fascinations of ferreting is that the element of surprise is never far away. Apart from stoats and weasels you may find rats coming out and even grey squirrels. One old jill retrieved, on separate occasions, a bat and a hibernating wren. I have also twice found pheasants down rabbit holes.

Training the Ferret

The work a ferret does is instinctive and you do not have to teach it to go down holes or look for rabbits. It is worth training it to respond to quiet sounds for food and to warn it that you are approaching. I click my tongue to let it know I am near, so that the albino ferret, half-blinded by the sudden daylight as it emerges, does not scoot back down the burrow as I loom over it. This is associated with feeding. I also squeak through pursed lips, vaguely like a rabbit squealing, to attract them. It helps entice them out of a hole.

Never grab a nervous, young ferret if it looks as though it is going to turn back into the warren. All this does is makes them hand-shy and start the aggravating habit of skulking. Always let them come out in their own time and let them sniff your hand to identify you. Pick them up very calmly.

Building tunnels and pipes, for your ferret to play in will get it fit and teach it to explore. Giving food at the lowest level will teach it to go down.

Stopping it Killing and Laying Up

All ferrets will kill if they can. It is the rabbit's job to make sure this does not happen. You can help by being quiet as you approach the warren. If the occupants hear you they will go very deep, making it hard to find and shift them. This is when they most usually get killed.

Ferrets kill for fun, so the fact that there is a dead rabbit below ground should not mean that the ferret will lay up. On the contrary it should carry on looking for more sport. What makes it stay with its kill is hunger or tiredness. Unless you are fond of digging I would advise you never to work a tired or hungry ferret. Mine always have food in front of them, both in the hutch and in the ferreting box. I also never work them for more than half a day, and usually I use two in the morning and a fresh two in the afternoon.

Trying to ferret out a rabbit you have chased into a hole is a recipe for disaster. Apart from being unsporting, it is counter-productive. The chased rabbit will have raced to the deepest part of the warren, thumping its feet in fear and alerting every other occupant that there is danger looming. While some of these may bolt, your good ferret will not rest until it has accounted for them all. The very last one, when the ferret is most tired, will be the one that you chased in. It will have balled itself up into a small furry boulder, blocking a narrow tunnel. In an attempt to move it the ferret scratches at its fur-clad backside, filling its claws with rabbit fur. After a while its feet resemble furry carpet slippers – and do little harm to the rabbit, which grimly remains hunched up. In this situation your ferret will eventually turn the rabbit but, if it kills it, will be so exhausted that it may lay up on the centrally heated carcass.

Falconry is not about numbers, although they seem important when we first start. If a rabbit beats your hawk to its hole, do not worry. Ferreting it there and then will be a lengthy and unrewarding process. Simply remember where this hole is for another time. If you fail to catch your quarry it will live to breed more like itself, and guarantee good sport for you in the future.

Individual ferrets can be true psychopaths. I had a sweet-natured jill, and have seen others, that would kill within seconds of entering a warren. They are a complete waste of time – give them away as pets, pass them on to someone who likes ratting, or have them put down. The one I had was entered to blue hare. On one occasion a hare ran for several hundred metres through the heather with the ferret clinging gamely to its neck. Another, killed by the hawk, had lost an eye to the ferret in the few minutes they had been together! I was glad that I was able to put that poor beast out of its misery.

Retrieving the Lost Ferret

Sometimes the best of ferrets will disappear for longer than you expect. Possibly the warren is more extensive or deeper than you first thought. Perhaps it has killed and got itself

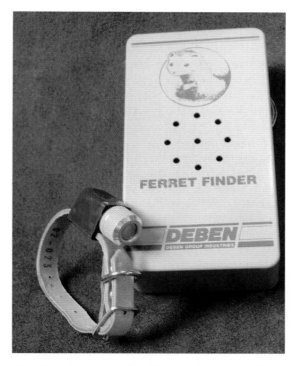

Ferret locator and collar. These help pinpoint the whereabouts of the ferret but encourage the ferreter to walk over the warren – so warning the rabbits and making the ferret's job harder.

trapped in a dead end behind its victim. You have no idea what has happened, so the constructive course of action is to do nothing for a bit longer. You know approximately where it is, and the chances are it is still working.

A lot of ferreters use **ferret locators**, small radio transmitters attached to a small collar, which send a signal to a handheld receiver. Because they have a locator available these characters are invariably impatient, or perhaps it is because they are impatient that they got it in the first place. At any rate they cannot resist stamping all over the warren to listen for the elusive bleep. Nothing is guaranteed to make a rabbit less likely to bolt than the sound of someone's size ten boots clomping about over its head.

Ferreting is about stealth and patience. Eventually you may have to approach the warren. Listen carefully at each hole and you may hear noises underground. Try to squeak the ferret up. If this does not work rattle your stick around the hole in an attempt to simulate the thumping of a rabbit's foot. Your ferret may come out to look for this new rabbit it has somehow overlooked. Equally you may be able to attract it by dangling another rabbit carcass down the hole.

If none of this works you may have to leave your ferret there. I sometimes do this but keep going back to check. Very often I see rabbits bolt and then the ferret reappears. It may or may not have blood around its chin (the sign that it has killed) but it has been working all the time. It is not unusual for this to happen more than an hour after you first put the ferret down.

The ferret that has truly laid up will not get up until late morning the next day. There is no need to rise at 'sparrow crack' to go and collect it. I find that putting a hob (male) ferret down the warren is the best way of stirring it up. The jills are not 'first thing in the morning' girls and will come out rather than stay with a randy male. Only if all this fails is it necessary to start digging, and that is the only time a locator is any use.

If you have lost a ferret it is always worth going back several times. I once found a lost jill in the same warren in which I had lost it three weeks before. They do not go far.

Lastly there are more wild polecats about than people realize. If you bear in mind that most captive ferrets are white, why is it that every dead ferret you see on the road is polecat coloured? I have had a jill dragged down a hole by an amorous polecat on one occasion, and I did have to dig her out.

Ferret Welfare

Since a good ferret is worth its weight in gold it make sense to look after it well. A dry, clean hutch is essential, with good hay for a bed and plentiful clean shavings to soak up any urine. Change soiled shavings daily to avoid smell. Ferrets have good toilet habits and will readily defecate in a tray.

Fresh water and good food are the only other things to worry about. I always feed my ferrets on flesh, mostly rabbit carcasses supplemented with day-old cockerels. The pellet foods that are now available are a convenience but that is all. My belief, from observation, is that ferrets fed on this tend to be bad to handle. Are they hyperactive through too many E numbers?

After a ferreting session check your ferrets over for ticks. Some areas are particularly prone to these. Mostly I just pull them out very quickly so that they do not have time to take a tight hold with their mouth. If they are firmly attached apply any sort of fat or grease around the tick so that it suffocates and lets go.

Security

Ferrets are great escapers. That pointed snout is used as a wedge to push open the smallest crack, and then the power in their sinuous bodies will drive them through – and they have the stamina to keep trying. It is important that your ferret hutch is really secure. If a ferret escapes it can, and will, find the nearest available hen house or rabbit hutch – with horrendous results.

Breeding

Jills should be taken out of season each year, as remaining in oestrus will cause health problems. Breeding is one way. Equally you can put her with a vasectomized hob to achieve matings that will convince her she is pregnant, or have her injected by your vet. Should you decide to go down the breeding route, be prepared for hefty food bills. Ferrets have huge litters (tens and twelves are not uncommon) and a growing litter of kits can attack a complete rabbit carcass like a shoal of piranhas. It only takes a short time to reduce one to a skeleton covered in skin. Feeding such a hungry horde is expensive and it can be hard to sell, or even give away, so many kits.

Carrying Boxes

I use plastic toolboxes from the DIY super-stores. Just pierce a few breathing holes in the sides with a hot point or a drill, add a strap to carry it with and you have a light, easily cleaned box. They are often brightly coloured, which is a useful aid if you mislay one – something that happens more frequently than you might think.

Wooden boxes tend to be too heavy for my liking. We have enough to carry. They do have an advantage over the plastic toolboxes in that they can be made sturdy enough to act as a portable step, to help you clamber over barbed wire fences and the like. You decide – it will be you that has to carry it.

DOGS

Dogs come in all shapes and sizes. Most are wolves at heart and can be used to flush game out. They will quickly understand the hawk's role in the matter, and even hard-mouthed killers will usually respect a hawk. I have seen a really tough Jack Russell work well with hawks and not go in on a kill, and my son had a lurcher that worked well on fox and hare, yet taught itself to point game for the birds. Moreover, although it would follow the hunt it made no attempt to join in the chase.

The majority of dogs will simply flush the game as they find it, bumping it up out of cover. Unfortunately they invariably flush it away from you and from the bird if it is on your fist. If your dog is very steady and works close to you (within the equivalent of a good-sized room) this may not be too bad. Admittedly you will need to be on 'red alert' all the time but you should get plenty of slips. Keep an eye on where the game has gone, and you can add another possible warren or bit of cover to the list of places to be flushed or ferreted on another occasion.

Useful Websites

For advice on all aspects of keeping ferrets refer to www.pakefieldferrets.co.uk, and for equipment go to www.deben.com.

Training Pointing Dogs

However, most serious hawkers and falconers will eventually want a pointing dog of some sort. Knowing where the game is before it takes off allows you the opportunity to position your bird in a place of maximum advantage. This may be on a high branch or still on your fist but with you standing on an elevated piece of ground. You can also decide to flush game away from the nearest cover, giving you a longer flight and the bird a greater chance of success. Very obviously this is a huge improvement. Unfortunately there is a price to pay. Pointing dogs can introduce a whole new level of stress to falconry.

These are all neurotic and hyperactive. They are driven 'obsessives' and believe in working vast swathes of land at dauntingly fast speeds. Getting them to work within the same parish is the initial challenge. Indeed you must recognize that containment rather than training is the first hurdle to overcome. Even then the problem does not become truly apparent until the dog gets into a game-rich environment.

At the training class or in the park there may be little to hint at the trouble in store for you. However, once its nose gets 'switched on', you will find its one brain cell and both ears get switched off. The heady scent of game fills its nostrils and it views the world through a kind of olfactory red mist. When this happens you may as well have ceased to exist. The need to suck up as much scent as possible is paramount. Unfortunately, as the dog ranges further and faster, it is gets physically beyond your control zone.

Basic Obedience

As always, prevention is better than cure. Introduce puppies to game scent from their

139

earliest days. At twelve weeks old they cannot run far and, if they do, are more likely to panic when they lose you. I would strongly recommend trying to achieve this when out exercising a puppy. Every time it is distracted I hide by dropping flat in long grass, climbing trees or simply changing direction and running away. The object is to teach the puppy to keep one eye on you all the time. Play on its insecurity to create a habit of attentiveness. When you do call it to you, do so in a stern voice or with a sharp blast of the whistle. Sound cross in order to work on its anxiety. However, as soon as it has actually got to you (not while it is on its way back) give unstinting praise.

This sounds the reverse of how the recall is taught in most dog training manuals. If those authors watched dogs doing the stay exercise (where a firm command is given to make the poor creature stay at a distance from its handler), they would see several edging forward. The stronger the command that is given the more dog feels it has done wrong, and needs to come to you for reassurance. Therefore, if you want the dog to come to you, it makes sense to tell it in an angry tone. Initially it may be frightened of the reception it will get, but once you give lavish praise when it does overcome its worries, it will come reliably and confidently every time. And that is the vital thing. The 'come' command, or whistle, must be non-negotiable. It is an imperative that the dog should never ignore.

Because you cannot second guess what a dog smells you are forced to believe it. Only by having good control of it in all other situations can you assume with any confidence that it is indeed working. It will give the appearance of rioting. Essential work commands for a pointing dog are 'come', 'turn' and 'stop'. Because of the distance at which the dog is working these will be whistled commands, often backed up by screams, threats and ranting.

'Turn' is, in my experience, a diluted version of the 'Come'. Rather than return directly to you the dog turns back from its previous direction and runs across you, thereby (it thinks) placating you while still continuing with its fun. If you practise this at right angles to a headwind, you will encourage your dog to develop a quartering pattern. The amount of 'outrun' you allow will depend on the nature of terrain you will be working. Dogs on grouse moors are expected to cover wider areas than dogs in woodland or small fields. Always permit more than you think you want. If your 'turn' command works and the dog is switched on to hawking, you can tighten the pattern up pretty easily.

Quartering can be taught in an enclosed area if you are fit enough. With your dog on a long line (up to 30m/100ft) you can steer it across your path. At the end of each sweep give the 'turn' whistle, followed immediately by a very sharp jerk. Do not give the dog time to obey. You want to keep it unsure and on tenterhooks to please you. The very second you have jerked it, you must compensate with loads of enthusiastic and genuine praise before running it in the opposite direction, still heaping praise on it. It can become something of a game. My present dog thinks being redirected is hilarious, and will yelp with glee at each change of direction I give him.

Chasing is a common fault with hawking dogs. They identify with your hawk or falcon, and when it chases are inclined to revert to pack behaviour by joining in. For this reason I tether my young dogs while ferreting, so that they cannot chase. If they try to they are brought up short by the sapling or fence post to which they are attached, but it has not been me that has corrected them. They learn the situation and come to believe that chasing is impossible. Similarly I try to put my dogs on the lead while they are on point, so that I can check them if they try to chase when the game is flushed. This means that my dogs can become 'sticky' on point and will not flush. No matter, it puts me in charge and I can choose which direction to flush game in.

It is much easier to prevent a bad habit developing than to curb it later.

'Stop' is a command that is used when you wish to redirect the dog. Used in conjunction with hand signals it can enable you to direct the dog to work areas you think it has missed. Experience has taught me that my dogs are more thorough than they seem. I have often made them work corners of land that I think they have missed, but invariably there is nothing there. You can teach redirection in the garden, with treats thrown to the indicated direction to reward its response.

Pointing

A dog points because it has found something or, in the case of a false point, thinks it has. They do not flush immediately because the pointing breeds of dog have an in-built anxiety level that makes them chronically indecisive. They want to chase but cannot. It is this insecurity that we exploit when we hide from the puppy to make it keep close.

Interestingly, a while ago I had a puppy that would roam out incredible distances. I am talking here of a four-month-old puppy being quite at ease about a kilometre away from me. I never managed to get her to keep close of her own accord, although I could achieve this with continual control. She also failed to point anything unless it was on the opposite side of an impassable fence. Her lack of insecurity was also responsible for the absence of the pointing reflex. When she was ten months old I was persuaded to sell her by a falconer who had been advised that some dogs took longer to point than others. He is still waiting!

When I got my first HPR (hunt, point, retrieve) dog I bought books on pointing dogs. They covered every aspect of rearing and training one could imagine – except how to teach the puppy to point! They were totally silent on this definitive aspect of the dog's work. The reason is that you cannot teach the puppy to point, it is an inherited behavioural trait. From an early age the puppy should

display a tendency to point both sights and scents. Breeders and books will tell you that this may take months and even years to develop. All I can say is that life is short. A puppy that is not showing signs of pointing by the time it is six months old is liable to be looking for a new home.

Developing the Point

It is possible to develop the pointing habit in dogs. Trainers sometimes use a partridge or pheasant wing suspended from a light cane or fishing rod. As the puppy approaches to investigate, this is whisked away. The puppy becomes intrigued but hesitant. It starts to check its approach at the anticipated 'vanishing' point. Praise reassures it that this is good behaviour. Sadly, as the puppy develops better vision and can follow the wing's movements, this training becomes impossible. It can be taught as a 'trick', but it is not a scent-inspired point.

Hiding caged quarry, for example a pet rabbit or tame pigeon, enables you to simulate a hunting exercise. The puppy can be worked towards the game on a long lead and be checked before it can go in and flush. Physically praising the dog, particularly by rubbing it gently, unbalancing it *towards* the quarry, will teach it to 'set' itself more solidly. Your tone of voice when praising for a point should be soothing and reassuring rather than exciting.

The False Point

The novice pointer owner will be over-aware of any hesitation his or her dog displays. There is a great temptation to encourage the dog to develop this into a proper point by telling it to 'steady', or even 'stay' if it comes to a brief halt. After all, you are worried the dog will flush the game before you get there, and you want it to have as many positive results as possible. The inexperienced dog that has been taught that staying on point is a good thing, and that wants to please you, will obligingly point the spot where it thought

The vertical point on squirrels. An experienced dog adds quarry species to its list as it learns what a hawk will catch.

What Will a Dog Point?

Dogs will instinctively point any gamey smell that is coming from a hidden source. Tight-sitting pheasants are pretty easy, as are rabbits that have clamped down in cover. Grouse and grey partridge I find quite easy, but the red-legged 'Frenchman' is a pain. It rarely sits tight and the dog will creep ever onwards after the scurrying covey. Woodcock and snipe have particularly elusive scent, so it is a red-letter day when we get a point on them.

My dogs have pointed a vast array of different game, adding to the list as they realize what the hawks will take. Squirrels, or at least the tree the squirrel went up, produce the vertical point, while pointing duck and moorhen causes problems for a swimming dog. I have had points on grass snakes and wild cat too.

Needless to say, my dogs diversify for their own ends. In summer they point ice creams, burgers, chips and so on!

Holding a Point

Once your dog is switched on to hawking and falconry it will hold a point for as long as you need. We were ferreting a very small warren, leaving my old bitch to continue working the hillside above her. She went on point some 30m (100ft) above us. Confident in her steadiness, and that our rabbit would bolt fairly quickly, we left her there while we waited for results. It took much longer than we thought, and in fact twenty-five minutes elapsed before the rabbit was accounted for. She held her point throughout and we got that one as well.

Age

The sooner the puppy is introduced to the hawking field the better. It will educate its nose and your eye, while watching it will alert you to changes in its behaviour and lead you to game. Why did it sniff that rabbit hole out of the dozens you have passed in a day? Because that is the warren that is occupied.

something might be. You, of course, lavish praise on it and then tell it to flush the non-existent game. It cannot, and you equally cannot correct it in case it thinks it is being told off for pointing when it was only trying to please. In future, if things are not going well and there is little game about, it may try to placate you by false pointing – didn't you teach it well!

Once your dog has demonstrated its willingness to point you should always encourage it gently forward if it hesitates. Use the same reassuring tone as you did when it first pointed. It will feel free to investigate a little more, either realizing there is nothing there or becoming more definite on the point.

Five months old and working already. The sooner you educate your pointing dog the better, but do not work it into the ground.

Back its judgement and be pleasantly surprised. Your praise will encourage it to be more definite another time.

Being out with you will teach it the routines that it will associate with hunting. It will also have to keep up, making it keep a watchful eye on you for fear of getting lost. This is a good way to teach it not to roam too far.

My current dog was taken out with his mother at three and a half months. What was intended to be an hour a day quickly became much more. His mother went lame and, with clients arriving, he had to work. In the end he worked a complete six-month season from the age of four months. I am not recommending that sort of workload, but he has an old head on his shoulders and is an exceptional worker. One might have expected his limbs to be affected but he has a very good hip score.

At the other end of the working life I had to retire his mother and grandmother at eight and nine years respectively. Both succumbed to injury as a result of too many miles on the clock, although both subsequently worked in a limited way if allowed. Perhaps the amateur hawker would get more years from a dog than I manage.

Breed

If you are exclusively working very open ground you may be suited by the English pointer or the English, Gordon, Irish or the Irish Red and White setters. All suffer selective deafness and are wide-ranging dogs. Only get one from proven working stock. If you have sufficient access to the sort of ground we are talking about, you should have the right contacts. If you have not got the right contacts it is because you have not got sufficient access to the sort of ground you need.

For mixed terrain you will be better suited by one of the hunt, point, retrieve group (the HPRs). There are an increasing variety of these coming on the market. The most common (and therefore the most likely to have recognized working lines) are the short-haired and wire-haired German pointers (GSPs and GWPs). A few long-coated German pointers are also emerging, which look quite promising (GLPs). The Brittany is the smallest (spaniel-sized) and most energetic of the common HPR breeds and can cope with any type of ground.

Hungarian vizlas, both smooth and wire-haired, are less common. They tend to be clingy and many do not seem to have the drive you may be looking for. However, they

143

English pointers are traditional grouse moor dogs.

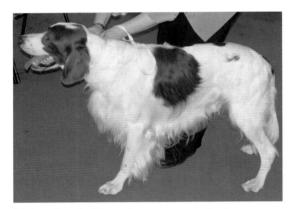

Irish red and white setters are a relatively new breed and have been developed for the show ring. Working specimens would be hard to find.

Irish setters are used quite often in their native land, so go there to find a good one.

Working English setters can be found but avoid the show strains, as they have been selected for other qualities.

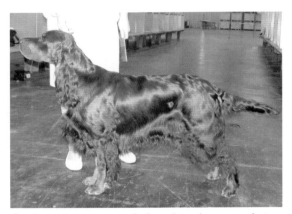

Gordon setters are rarely found on the moors but some individuals will work well.

are pretty biddable. Weimeraners are usually not good workers as they have been bred mostly for show, though there may be exceptions. Large Munsterlanders are not yet present in enough numbers to allow for a fair appraisal. The Italian spinone is the largest HPR breed and can be very steady, so that a point can sometimes be hard to distinguish from the natural movement of the dog! Sheep

One of the most popular falconry dog breeds, the short-haired German pointer will work in open and wooded country.

Long-haired German pointers are just starting to make a name for themselves and seem quieter and more easily controlled than the short- and wire-haired varieties.

The wire-haired German pointer is a bit tougher than its short-haired cousin and the dogs should be avoided by first-time handlers.

The Hungarian vizla is the only breed that is all one colour, including the eyes and nose. They are very sensitive and can cling too close if you over-discipline them at the start.

are particularly unbothered by spinones. 'Is that a sheep or a Spinone on point?'

Most HPR breeds are rare. To some extent this is a reflection on the British obsession with driven shooting, which has no place for this less productive way of finding game. However, you should be wary of any breed that is not common. Has it got vices that make it difficult in some way or another? The answer with all HPR breeds is 'yes'. They all need a great amount of exercise. They all suffer from insecurity and need constant reassurance (which is jolly flattering for the first ten minutes but very wearing after that). They are difficult to leave, either in a kennel, your car or your house.

The Brittany is frequently used by falconers and is a versatile dog. For their size they have formidable energy levels and can cope with all sorts of cover. They can be headstrong and need firm handling from the outset but are very friendly and a convenient size.

The Italian spinone is a large and heavily built dog that is prone to selective deafness. It works comparatively slowly, and is not gaining much popularity, which throws up warning signs.

The large Munsterlander is an attractive dog but has a strong tendency to hunt game rather than pointing it. Best avoided unless you really want one.

There may be health problems in the various breeds. Is hip displasia a problem, or epilepsy? What is their normal life expectancy?

Be objective in deciding which breed and sex is right for you. Will it fit in your home? Is the breed good with children? Is there a history of aggression in the breed? Will your wife be able to exercise it? Go and watch the different breeds working.

Once you have decided which breed to get, you need to find someone with a good, working bitch they are intending to breed from. If this proves impossible then find who owns the fathers of any good workers you have seen. Ask the stud dog owner if any working bitch has been mated to his dog recently. Always insist on parents of proven working stock and remember that breeders are selling puppies. They will always claim their stock works well. Ask for telephone numbers of previous customers who are working their stock so that you can do your own research.

Hawking Dogs Versus Shooting Dogs

With the more common breeds of HPRs there are some kennels that specialize in working dogs. At first sight this looks as if they will be the answer to your needs. However, if they breed dogs for the shooting field, they may not produce the qualities you are looking for.

The most common vices of hawking dogs are a tendency to chase and a selective deafness. The physical chase by the hawk as the game is flushed encourages the dog to revert to pack behaviour and join in. This visual chase and the pack situation are absent in the shooting field. Moreover, the shooting man has the advantage of a loud bang to get the dog's attention. This suggests the falconer should look for a more sensitive type of dog, with more acute hearing. It will be easier to control and stop.

The shooting fraternity often fails to grasp the needs of the falconer. Shooting dogs need to be good retrievers and steady to shot. We need neither of these. Equally we do not want what the shooting fraternity rejects, that is, hard-mouthed, riotous thugs. Their rejects that we do want are the gun-shy ones that are too sensitive or the ones that will not retrieve, that is, that have not got a strong chasing instinct.

There are few hawking bloodlines to go on. Individual falconers have good individual dogs. If you know the virtues you are looking for and are prepared to do your homework and choose the right mating, you may well get the perfect dog.

Coping With Livestock

Your hawking dog is going to be running across farmland that carries livestock. You should specifically get it used to all sorts of poultry and sheep, cattle and horses. Do this when the puppy is young as it will be more easily intimidated by livestock at that age. Keep it on the lead at first.

At the risk of upsetting breed enthusiasts I feel this aspect of the dog's work is particularly important with males of the German pointer and large Munsterlander breeds.

HORSES

Occasionally I am asked if it possible to hawk from horseback. People can get very close to game when out riding, and the idea of flying a hawk or falcon from horseback is very attractive. Unfortunately the logistics are against you.

In 1839 the Old Hawking Club moved its headquarters to Loo in Holland because Salisbury Plain was getting too cut up with fences to enable members to follow the falcons on horse. Over 160 years later you can bet that it has not got any easier. Riding fast across open country demands that you keep an eye on the ground in front of you, not up in the air. Those who claim to do horseback hawking and falconry have staff with four-wheel-drive vehicles and telemetry to reunite the field with the falcon at the end of the day. It is impractical for the individual falconer.

Horses could be used for hare hawking in very open country. It would certainly simplify the problem of carrying such heavy game. Hawking from horseback in any country that requires jumping would be disastrous. A mount that can jump a ditch and a hedge from a virtual standstill will be unlikely to stand still in the middle of an open field while you attend to the hawk and the kill. There is also the difficult problem of remounting with a hawk on your fist, or would you remount and then call the hawk to the fist?

One falconer told me that he exercised his hawks from horseback but admitted that he did not hunt them in this way. He found that the hawks had a tendency to try to land on the horse's head. He also admitted that he never went out alone but always had a mounted companion, who could hold his horse if he needed to get off to attend to his hawk.

Some horses are nervous of birds of prey, while most will come to accept them. About one in ten really like the birds.

Glossary

Accipiter True short-winged hawks, that is, sparrowhawks, goshawks, Cooper's hawks, etc.

Astroturf Synthetic grass material used for perch surfaces. Its texture allows air to circulate and it provides a cushioned surface.

Austringer A person who flies hawks as opposed to falcons.

Aylmeri A jessing system, designed originally by Guy Aylmer, in which permanent anklets and interchangeable mews and hunting jesses replace the traditional jesses.

Bate Any attempt by the bird to get to, at or from anything while on the perch or fist.

Beams Old-fashioned term for the primary feathers.

Bechins Small rewards of food, morsels or beakfuls.

Bells Attached to the hawks legs, tail or (less commonly) neck to aid its location on a kill. A pair of bells should have slightly differing tones to give greater effect.

Bewits Tiny leather straps for fastening leg bells.

Bind to The action of catching and holding quarry or a lure in the air or on the ground.

Block The flat-topped perch given to falcons to simulate a rock. May be topped with cork, Astroturf, etc.

Blood 1. 'In blood' refers to growing feathers. 2. That portion of the hawk or falcon's diet that is of very red meat.

Bolt 'To fly at bolt' refers to slipping an accipiter at quarry.

Bow The simulated branch provided for any tree-perching raptor, particularly hawks. May be leather-covered or have rope or Astroturf surface.

Bowse To drink (also booze, bouze, etc.).

Brail A soft sling of leather or cloth that immobilizes the butt of the wing and stops an injured or frightened bird bating.

Brancher A young hawk or falcon that is exploring the immediate environs of its nest.

Break into The act of actually devouring quarry after killing and plucking.

Cadge A frame on which several hawks can be carried at a time. Used around the body over open country or in vehicles. Also **cadger**, **cadge man/boy**, referring to who carried the cadge.

Call off To whistle or lure a bird from a perch or, with particularly obedient birds, from an unsuitable chase.

Carrying 1. The vice when a hawk flies away with its quarry instead of permitting your approach. 2. The taming process involving the bird spending extensive periods on the fist.

Cast 1. To hold a bird bodily for examination, coping, belling, etc. 2. To produce a pellet or casting. 3. Two hawks flown together.

Casting The regurgitated pellet of undigested fur or feather which serves to clean the crop out.

Cast off To release, particularly a falcon, for free flight (*see* **Slip**).

Cawking time Pairing-up time.

Cere The exposed flesh at the base of the beak in which the **nares** are situated.

Check To fly at check is when a bird switches quarry in mid-pursuit.

Cope To trim overgrown beaks or talons with a knife, file, emery board or even snippers.

Crabbing When a hawk attacks another when flying in a **cast**.

Craye A digestive ailment.

Creance The light line on which the bird is trained before it is flown loose.

Creche-Reared A captive-bred bird that has mostly been reared away from its parents but in the company of siblings or a peer group.

Crines The short, hair-like feathers around the **cere**.

Croaks A respiratory disease.

Crop 1. The skin 'bag' in the hawk's neck, which forms the first reservoir for food and where initial digestion takes place. 2. The amount of food given to a hawk in one meal; for example, 'how much crop have you given it?' A bird which has been gorged is said to have a 'full crop'.

Deck feathers The central two tail feathers.

Enseam To get a hawk into flying condition after the seasonal moult.

Enter To introduce a hawk successfully to quarry.

Eyass A young bird still in the nest or **eyrie**. Throughout its subsequent life it will still be known as an eyass bird.

Falcon 1. Generically any species of long-winged bird of prey. 2. The female of any such species. 3. Specifically the female peregrine.

Feake The action of wiping or stropping the beak on the perch to clean it.

Fed up When the bird has eaten and can no longer be expected to work.

Festoon The curved side of a hawk's beak.

Food imprint A hawk that has been hand-reared and perceives people as potential parents. Associated with screaming and undesirable aggression towards the falconer.

Foot To strike at or clutch with the feet.

Fret marks Lines of weakness across feathers, indicating hunger or stress at that stage in the feather's development, sometimes called **hunger traces**.

Frounce A disease of the mouth and nostrils.

Full-summed When a bird's new feathers are all finished growing and have hardened off – more commonly called **hard-penned**.

Furniture Falconry equipment.

Gorge To allow the hawk to eat as much as it wants, that is, until it is full.

Hack A planned period of liberty for untrained and unentered eyasses which simulates their natural development. They are allowed freedom to range and so develop strength, flying and hunting skills and establish a territory. Hack ends when the eyass first kills or is thought to be very close to this success. The purpose is to produce a bird as close to its wild cousin as possible. Rarely done nowadays because of the financial value of birds and the greater dangers, such as power lines, traffic and shooters.

Hack back As above, but continuing until the bird has resumed independent living in the wild. Used particularly in rehabilitation of injured or immature wild stock.

Haggard Thought to be the optimum bird. A haggard is a mature wild bird with honed hunting skills.

Halsband 1. A light strap placed around the hawk's neck, particularly with accipiters, to act as a slingshot and thus propel the bird forward from the fist (also Jangaoli in the Orient). 2. A light strap, often of elastic, for fixing a neck bell to a hawk.

High Describes a hawk that is overweight.

Hood 1. The leather cap that covers the hawk's eyes and keeps it calm. The most common types are Anglo-Indian, Bahreini and Dutch. 2. The act of placing the hood on the bird's head.

Hood-shy Describes a hawk that evades the hood. Caused by an ill-fitting hood or by clumsy introduction to the hood. The fault can be remedied with time and patience.

Imp To repair broken feathers by splicing the two halves together with imping needles, traditionally made of triangular-sectioned iron needles steeped in brine. Now guitar strings or carbon-fibre splinters are used.

Imprinting The process by which a young bird identifies its parents or people. There are varying degrees of advantages and disadvantages (*see* **creche-reared**, **food im-print**, **social imprint**, **screamer** and **parent-reared**).

Intermewed A bird that has been moulted in captivity (in the **mews**). With the modern dependence on captive-bred birds the term is largely obsolete and birds are simply referred to by their actual age, that is, five years old, rather than by the number of times they have been through the moult, that is four times intermewed.

Jack The male merlin and therefore Europe's smallest falcon.

Jerkin The male gyrfalcon.

Jesses The leather straps around the hawk's legs by which it is tied up.

Jokin Sleeping.

Leash The braided rope or nylon tether by which a hawk is tied. Formerly made of oiled rawhide or similar.

Lure 1. The imitation quarry used to recall a hawk or teach it footing skills. May be a swung lure or a ground lure (dummy bunny). 2. The act of using a lure for training, recalling or exercising a hawk.

Mail A hawk's breast feathers.

Make To completely train a bird. A made hawk is the finished article.

Make-hawk An old, experienced hawk flown with a novice hawk to encourage or teach it.

Make in To approach a hawk on a kill or the lure.

Make point When a hawk throws up over the spot where quarry has disappeared into cover.

Man The process of familiarizing the hawk with the things of mankind (*see* **carrying**).

Mantle To shield the quarry or food from view by spreading wings over it.

Mar-hawk 1. A hawk spoilt by a bad falconer. 2. A bad falconer.

Mew To put a bird in the mews to moult.

Mews The building in which the bird is kept.

Musket The male sparrowhawk and Europe's smallest accipiter. Gave its name to the gun.

Mutes The faeces of a bird of prey.

Nares The nostrils of a bird of prey.

Parent-reared A hawk that has been solely reared by its parents and may be expected to be free of the vices associated with imprinting. It may also be wilder and slower to tame.

Passage hawk A bird that has been trapped in immature plumage, but after it has left the eyrie.

Petty singles The toes of a hawk.

Pitch The height individual falcons will mount to before **waiting on**. Will vary with fitness and condition.

Plume To pluck feathered quarry.

Put in To enter cover – applies to hawk or quarry.

Put out Drive quarry from cover.

Put over The emptying of the crop as its contents are moved to the stomach.

Pounces The talons of a short-winged hawk.

Quarry Whatever the hawk chases.

Rake off To drift away and lose interest in the falconer and the chase.

Rangle Small stones inserted in the hawk's crop in the mistaken belief that they broke up internal fat and aided weight loss.

Reclaim Used to denote the process of re-training a hawk which has not been handled for any reason, e.g. the moult.

Red hawk An immature hawk. Traditional species like peregrines and goshawks change from brown(red) plumage to blue in their second year.

Ring perch Similar to a bow perch but consists of a ring on edge, topped with padding, mounted on a single spike of variable height. The centre of the ring is solid or taped across to prevent the bird passing through it.

Ring up To climb in spirals, either by thermalling or by sustained flight.

Robin A male hobby (*Falco subbuteo*).

Rouse To shake the feathers, often prior to flight.

Sails Outstretched wings, particularly when a hawk sets its wings to soar or wait on.

Sarcel The outermost primary feather.

Screamer *see* **food imprint**.

Screen perch A free-standing bar perch, usually at waist level, with a screen of sacking or carpet hung tautly below to aid the hawk's efforts to climb back after a bate. Dangerous for unfit, ill or young birds.

Seclusion aviary Aviary built specifically for breeding, with solid sides to prevent visual disturbance during the breeding cycle.

Seel The Eastern practice, probably now obsolete, of sewing a newly trapped hawk's eyelids together to save using a hood.

Serve The falconer's role in falconry. To produce game under the hawk.

Sharp set Hungry.

Slices The droppings of accipiters, hawks, eagles and buzzards.

Slip release, particularly an accipiter, at quarry.

Social imprint A hawk that has been reared away from its parents and in human company, but who has not been allowed to associate people with food. Very tame and better behaved than food imprints. Unlikely to breed.

Stoop The steep dive of a falcon from its pitch. Speeds up to 560kph (350mph) have been recorded.

Strike To strike the hood refers to loosening the hood braces in preparation for removing it. Refers mostly to birds flown out of the hood, that is, carried in the field with the hood on and only slipped once quarry is in view.

Swivel A freely revolving brass or steel link to which the jesses are fastened, and which also accommodates the leash. Stops the jesses getting too twisted.

Take stand To perch in a tree, sometimes for a better vantage, more discouragingly to roost or sulk.

Telemetry Radio tracking equipment where the bird carries a small transmitter which the falconer can locate with a directional receiver.

Throw up When a hawk swings up into the air on losing sight of its quarry, often in readiness for a second attack.

Tiercel 1. Definitively a male peregrine. 2. Tiercel gos(hawk). 3. The male of any middle to large falcon.

Tirings Tough, non-nourishing pieces of food given to exercise and occupy a bird that is not being flown. Helps to trim beaks and often given the day following a gorge.

Train The tail of a hawk.

Varvels A small, flat ring fastened at the end of the jesses through which the leash could be passed. Not in use now.

Waiting on A trained hawk or falcon circling overhead, anticipating being **served** by the falconer.

Wake or watch When the falconer deprives a new hawk of sleep to accelerate its training.

Warble To stretch the wings and simultaneously spread the tail. Often prior to **rousing**.

Weather To place the hawk out in the open.

Weathering ground A specific sheltered area in which the hawk is weathered.

Yarak Describes the condition of a hawk that is fit and ready to hunt.

Useful Information

ORGANIZATIONS

DEFRA (Department for the Environment, Food & Rural Affairs) is responsible for implementing statutory requirements for wildlife and the countryside. It registers all 'sensitive' British birds of prey, issues Article 10 certificates for the commercial use of European species of birds of prey on behalf of the EU, and also issues import and export licences on all animal and plant species under the CITES (Convention on International Trade in Endangered Species) agreement.
Floor 1, Zone 17, Temple Quay House,
2 The Square, Bristol BS1 6EB
Tel: 0117 372 8691
Fax: 0117 372 8206
www.defra.gov.uk

IBR (Independent Bird Register) is a professional service enabling falconers to obtain closed rings for captive-bred birds and split rings for unringed birds or birds ringed by other organizations. The IBR rings have a unique serial number and a central telephone number to facilitate the tracing and return of lost birds of prey. They maintain a register of bird ownership and supply government-approved documentation. This service is world- wide.
Tel: 0870 60 88 500
www.ibr.org.uk
IAF The International Association for Falconry and Conservation of Birds of Prey.
www.gyrcross.freeserve.co.uk

IOS The International Owl Society
www.members.tripod.co.uk/IOS

AECCA Spanish Association for Falconry and Conservation of Raptors.
Email RABAGU@teleline.es

Raptor Rescue
Tel: 0870 241 0609
www.raptorrescue.org.uk

International Falconer Quarterly magazine
www.intfalconer.com

Other falconry clubs Try
www.falconclubs.fsnet.co.uk

North America
NAFA North American Falconers Association www.n-a-f-a.org

US State Fish & Wildlife Departments The government agency to whom initial application for an apprentice falconer permit must be made.
www.fws.gov

US Falconry Apprenticeship This is dependent on you first obtaining sponsorship from an existing general or master falconer and then obtaining your apprentice permit as above. There is a theoretical examination to be passed, plus an inspection of your facilities and equipment before a licence will be issued to trap a hawk. In most states this would be a red-tailed hawk. After a further two years' experience the apprentice will then be upgraded to a general falconry licence – permitting him to trap and keep an additional bird.

California Hawking Club Look on their website for the apprentice manual and study guide on passing the apprenticeship examination.
www.calhawkingclub.org

Recommended Reading

There are hundreds of books on falconry, in most languages and from different periods of falconry. The titles listed below are those most generally available and used by modern falconers.

In the UK the **IBR Falconry Directory** is the must-have handbook for any potential falconer. It lists breeders, clubs, falconry centres, equipment manufacturers, suppliers of aviary materials, specialist veterinary surgeons, raptor insurance agencies, display presenters, pest controllers, dog breeders and trainers, ferret supplies, art and book dealers, gifts, hawking holidays, microchipping, raptor rescue organizations, taxidermists and telemetry manufacturers. It also has regular updates on statutory requirements and changes, and is interspersed with articles of general or specific interest for falconers. Allied to it is an internet advertising site, **IBR Birdmart**.
www.ibr.org.uk

Beebe, Frank L., *A Falconry Manual* (Hancock House, 1984; ISBN 0 88839 978 2)

Ford, Emma, *Falconry: Art and Practice* (Cassell, 1996; ISBN 0 7137 2588 5)

Fox, Nick, *Understanding the Bird of Prey* (Hancock House, 1995; ISBN 0 88839 317 2)

Glasier, Philip, *Falconry & Hawking* (Batsford, 1998; ISBN 0 7134 0232 6)

Kimsey, Bryan and Hodge, Jim, *Falconry Equipment: A Guide to Making and Using Falconry Gear* (Kimsey & Hodge, 2002)

Oakes, William C., *The Falconer's Apprentice – A Guide to Training a Red-tail Hawk* (Eagle Wing, 2001)

Parry-Jones, Jemima, *Training Birds of Prey* (David & Charles, 2001)

Index

poaching 108
poisons 54, 55, 70, 115

quarry 23, 125, 126–133
   licenses 126, 133
   species 16, 126–133

rangle *see* feeding
rickets 72

scales *see* weight control
screaming *see* imprint vices
serving the bird 110–114
   beating 102, 112, 127
   flushing 112–114
   self-hunting 111, 130
   stalking 111
   still-hunting 26, 66
short-wings 25–28
Smith, Richard 33
stick 50, 128, 130, 133
sticky footed 102, 116
stoop 17, 98
Summers, Gerald 52
swivels 44, 74–75

tail mounts 46–47
talons *see* health care – feet
telemetry 16, 45–47
thermalling 17; *see also* hawking hazards
thiamine 26
tiercel 112
tirings 55
travelling box 41, 71
trespass 108

veterinary surgeons 63, 68, 69
vultures 15, 30

weathering 12
   ground *see* housing
weight control 53, 63, 64, 72, 91–94
   flying weight 91–92, 111
   food intake 54, 80–81, 92–94, 96
   gorging 25, 54, 93
   scales 50
   weighing 79
whistle 86
White, T.H. 27
Williams, Mike 68
wingtip oedema 118